THE THEOMACHIA

THE THEOMACHIA

A Trilogy

BY

WILLIAM CHARLES BELLER

HORIZON PRESS

1961

Manufactured in the United States of America

CONTENTS

In grateful acknowledgment to Sara Clyne for her invaluable assistance in editing the manuscript of THE THEOMACHIA and in seeing it through the many other steps from manuscript to printed page.

WCB

DEDICATION

Ye unknown, high, mysterious Powers,
    Who rule the sacred thought of man:
The fruit of many holy hours
    Pays tribute to your wisdom's plan.
My works are yours, for by your grace,
    Unseen, unknown, all blessings are,
Like tidings from a secret place,
    Or beacon of a guiding star.
I know my works, but not your ways,
    Nor yet what purposes unguessed,
Have led me on these many days
    To follow your implied behest.
I know not if the verse I write
    By my own human skill is wrought,
Or whether some transcendent might
    But moulds to shape my passive thought.
So take these works: for all their faults
    On me alone shall rest the blame.
If aught sublime their theme exalts,
    Yours be the triumph and the fame.
So be they Yours, where'er they go,
    My Masters, whom I reverence still—
That Your Own Selves I yet may know,
    That I may better do Your will.

AUTHOR'S PREFACE

THE PRESENT work owes its inception, primarily, to my admiration for the Greek drama as an art-form, and my desire to produce an original work in this genre.

The classical Greek drama differs from other forms of poetic drama chiefly in the observance of the so called dramatic unities of Time, Place, and Action, and in the part played by the chorus. The unity of time implies that the action portrayed shall all occur in the time of the actual stage production; there are no "flashbacks" to past time, or lapses of time between acts or scenes. The unity of place implies that there shall be no shifts of scene, that all the action portrayed shall occur in the location represented by a single stage setting, and that any relevant action supposed to occur elsewhere shall be narrated either by the characters themselves or by messengers introduced for this specific purpose. The unity of action implies that only one significant event shall be dramatically portrayed; there shall be no minor or subsidiary plots beside the central theme.

Another peculiarity is that not more than three speaking actors shall appear on the stage at the same time, though the chorus, or the leader thereof, can take part in the dialogue in addition to these. The chorus has three principal functions: it may comment on the action, it may describe events invisible to the audience, and it may communicate with the actors in various circumstances. There are no curtains or intermissions between acts; instead the acts are separated by choric odes which are lyrical poems having a specific metrical structure, to wit: First there is the *strophe*, a stanza or group of stanzas expressing a certain lyrical statement. This is followed by the *antistrophe*, which repeats the exact verse-pattern of the *strophe*, but which may express a sense antithetic or antiphonal to it. Finally, the *epode* follows a different verse-pattern, and may express the resolution of the thesis and antithesis of the *strophe* and *antistrophe*.

Greek scholars offer ingenious and probably correct explanations of the origin of these conventions, but their sole significance from an aesthetic standpoint is that they give the work a unity, simplicity, and symmetry, comparable to the lines of a Greek temple, and supremely satisfying to those who have acquired a taste for it. The rigid formal limitations also provide an intriguing challenge to the ingenuity of the author.

My own admiration of this art-form dates from my school days, in 1915, when I witnessed a production of *Iphigenia in Tauris*, in Gilbert Murray's translation, under the direction of Granville Barker. I then began to read all the examples of Greek drama I could find in English literature. Some time later, I came across a statement in a work on Greek poetry to the effect that if the Greeks had attempted to give artistic expression to the influence on human thought of the transition from paganism to Christianity, they might have expressed it in terms of a dramatic conflict between the Olympian and the Christian Gods. Suddenly the idea struck me to produce an original work along these lines. But it seemed to me necessary to depict both the antecedent causes and the consequences of that conflict, so the projected work assumed the form of a trilogy or series of three dramas, such as the Greeks themselves were accustomed to present, in which the crucial event or crisis occurred in the second drama. The whole would be a philosophical allegory of the evolution of man's conception of Deity. I decided to call it the *Theomachia*, a word borrowed from the twentieth book of the Iliad, meaning "The Battle of the Gods"; the Gods who battle are, of course, man's ideas and ideals of Deity.

As the work progressed, I came to the realization that what overthrew paganism, destroyed the classical civilization, and ruled the Western world during the "Dark Ages" was not so much Christianity or the spirit of Christ, as it was the spirit of fanaticism, obscurantism, and authoritarianism. This spirit I personified as the character Phantasmus, a name chosen to indicate its shadowy and illusory nature. It goes without saying that nothing I have written here or elsewhere is intended as an attack on Christianity, or, for that matter, on the truth of any religion.

About three-quarters of the work was completed prior to 1919, but it was not until 1952 that the entire work was completed.

In the development of the work, I have taken certain liberties both with the legend and with the dramatic form. It should be remembered that even among the ancient Greeks themselves, the content of certain mythical legends was never definitely fixed, but was somewhat modified by each succeeding author. So, for purposes of my own allegory, I chose to omit references to the War Between the Gods and the Giants, and to transfer to the War Between the Gods and the Titans certain episodes usually associated with the other war. I have also ignored the legend that man had originally possessed fire, but had lost it during Deucalion's Flood, after which it was restored to him by Prometheus; and I assumed what to me seems more dramatic and more significant allegorically, that as a result of Prometheus' act he acquired a new power he had never previously possessed.

As regards the art-form, I believe I have observed implicitly the unities of place and action, and the convention as regards the number of speakers. The only liberty I have taken with regard to the unity of time is that in the third drama the time-scale may be considered somewhat expanded, as befits the actions of superhuman beings; that is to say, a few hours of stage-time in the lives of the Gods may represent a much longer period among mortal men on earth.

The first drama observes the classical conventions strictly; in the second and third I take some liberties in the use of the choruses. In the final chorus, I depart from the strict strophe, antistrophe, epode structure, still, however, retaining the general antiphonal pattern. The expedient of introducing two, and later three choruses, has, as far as I am aware, no classical precedent. I employed it because, as will be explained presently, each chorus presents a distinct point of view, and the development of the ideological structure of the work required the recurrence of these several viewpoints.

In diction, style, and metrical structure, I was guided by my own sense of the appropriate, seeking rather *le mot juste* than straining after novelty and ostentatious originality. The same considerations governed my use of archaisms, and the recurrence of certain phrases.

The subject matter of the work is the battle of ideas, the ideas which are the "Gods" that rule men. These ideas are expressed symbolically, not by a simple verbal symbolism, but by their personification as characters whose qualities, origins, and destinies are revealed by their words and actions. The various mythologies and religions are but elements in a system of symbolism, none of which possesses a validity intrinsically greater than any other. One's choice among them is governed entirely by personal preference and aesthetic considerations. Having chosen the Greek drama as an art-form, it is consistent with artistic unity to prefer the symbolism of Greek mythology to an eclecticism which might seem of more universal import; yet this eclecticism and the interchangeability of symbolic elements is implicit throughout, and made explicit in certain passages.

It was my original hope to maintain strict scientific accuracy in the cosmology and technology of the work, but the rapid progress of science made this impossible. Allusions to contemporary theories became obsolete almost before they were written down. I therefore attempted fidelity to the spirit of science, combined with a judicious vagueness deliberately observed in matters of specific detail. The same is true, to a slightly lesser degree, as regards political and sociological allusions.

I have always held that a poem must speak for itself as a unique expression of an author's aesthetic experience. If it fails to communicate this, it fails in its mission. If it were possible to communicate the author's meaning more clearly or completely in prose, then prose rather than verse should be the preferred medium of the original literary effort. Still, others have felt that a brief explanation of the significance of the chief characters and a synopsis of action would be of value.

The central theme of the work may be described as the Apotheosis of Man, to be achieved through the complete spiritualization of his nature. The three choruses, and the several protagonists become the spokesmen for different aspects of human thought and feeling, enacted against a background of Cosmic evolution. The Spirits of Cosmic Forces are spokesmen of an outlook in general accord with present-day scientific theories. They are the Voice of Science, expressive of reality on the phenomenal or perceptual level. The Angels are the spokesmen of man's devotional nature, and as such, while capable of stooping to superstition and fanaticism, are ready enough to recognize Truth, as it is revealed to them. They are the Voice of Religion, expressive of reality on the emotional level. The Muses are at first the spokesmen of classical Greek philosophy, later of a more universal philosophy or rationalistic world-picture. They are the Voice of Philosophy, expressive of reality on the intellectual level. The synthesis of the three is the Voice of Wisdom, expressive of reality on the spiritual level, reality on a super-rational or super-intellectual level, in short, absolute or ultimate reality.

Cronus and Rhea, whose names mean Time and Flux, are the parents of all the Gods; they represent the primordial process from whence all concrete objectivity emerges. Cronus as Time, devours his own offspring, until tricked into releasing them. He symbolises the brute power of nature, human thought on a primitive level. Zeus represents mentality, expressed first as sheer cunning, later made compassionate by suffering. Prometheus, whose name means Forethought, is primarily reason, shown under various aspects as prudent foreknowledge, science, advanced technology, and the like. Phantasmus is the spectre evoked by priestcraft to terrify the ignorant, the extra-cosmic personal god substituted for the God within, man's own Higher Self. Pallas symbolises at first the highest rational synthesis of Greek philosophy, later Wisdom, in its most universal and transcendental aspect.

In the first drama, the chorus chanting alone in the darkness strikes the keynote in an ode descriptive of the process of cosmic evolution. Prometheus, with foreknowledge of impending disaster, "interrogates nature" in the person of the chorus, as to his course of action, but succeeds only in confirming his own suspicions. Cronus is challenged by the emergence of mentality, Zeus, but fails to meet the challenge because he spurns the counsel of reason, Prometheus, and relies on brute force alone. Zeus, on the other hand, hearkens to the counsel of reason, and becomes master of the thunderbolt by learning the secret of controlling electricity, the key to all natural forces. By this he overcomes the Titanic powers of primordial nature.

But Zeus refuses to recognise man's evolutionary destiny, and seeks to destroy the human race. Prevented by his oath from taking direct action against it, he pronounces a curse against man, dooming him to become the slave of an adverse environment. To counteract this, Prometheus brings man the divine fire, thereby conferring upon him the means of technological mastery of his environment. To punish Prometheus for this act, Zeus sentences him to be bound to the rock of material existence. But man's survival is assured, and the chorus of Cosmic Forces chants the paean of man's ultimate mastery of the material world.

In the second drama, Zeus has outgrown his youthful arrogance and is toiling as a benevolent ruler to foster the progress of the human race. But the consequences of his sins against reason and against man remain: Because he sought to enslave reason, it will not serve him in his need; and because of his curse, man has become the sort of being capable of worshipping an irrational god. The wisest and holiest of men is crucified, and in his place arises a stupendous Phantom of Unreason, before whom the Gods of Olympus go into exile.

In the third and concluding drama, the Phantom of Unreason sits on the throne of heaven, surrounded by servile flatterers. They relate the fantastic fable of a universe created out of nothing, of an unevolving nature maintained by miracles, and of a human race blasted by the curse of an original sin from which it can be saved only through a supernatural process of vicarious atonement. But the divine fire bestowed by Prometheus continues to burn in the minds of men who, as ages pass, begin to doubt the dogmas inculcated by priestcraft, and to use their own God-given powers to wrest from nature itself the secrets of reality. The Phantom of Unreason rallies his forces to do battle with mankind, but his hosts wither before the lightnings of Truth, and he himself fades into nothingness. The Gods of Reason, Truth, and Wisdom return from exile, but refuse to re-assume their lordship over mankind, which has by this time won the right to freedom and to absolute mastery of its own destiny.

The above is but one meaning of my allegory, and it should be borne in mind that it is the virtue of an allegory to have a number of different meanings at the same time, all equally true.

WILLIAM C. BELLER

New York
March, 1961.

xvi

PROMETHEUS THE COUNSELLOR

A LYRICAL DRAMA

DRAMATIS PERSONAE

Prometheus	*A Titan*
Cronus	*A Titan*
Hyperion	*A Titan*
Iapetus	*A Titan*
1st Messenger	
Zeus	*A son of Cronus*
Poseidon	*A son of Cronus*
2nd Messenger	
Kratos	*A follower of Zeus*
Rhea, Oceanus and other Titans	
Hephaestus, Hades, and other Gods	
Chorus	*Spirits of Cosmic Forces*

Scene: A barren, rocky summit.

The action commences shortly before dawn.

Time: The remote past.

1

PROMETHEUS THE COUNSELOR

(Scene opens with stage in darkness with a backdrop of stars)

First Chorus   Sisters, how fare the worlds? The stars
        Float through the sable sea of night;
And far beyond the gloom, which bars

THEY MUSE
UPON THE
VASTNESS OF
THE COSMOS

        The searchings of our yearning sight,
More worlds, more stars, seen by the mind
        Move on in the great cosmic dance.
What mighty laws their motions bind
        Through birth and death, through change and chance!

They fare as is their wont to do:
        They move to the vast cosmic chime
Unchanging ever, though a few

THEY REFLECT
UPON THE
IMPERMANENCE
OF ITS
CONSTITUENT
PARTS

        Grow sick and weary with the time.
They sink from sight and fade away,
        But others in their places rise
And shine their hour, and decay,
        In endless cycles of the skies.
Change ever, and yet still unchanged
        The Whole remains, though parts may fall;
Fixed amid endless flux, arranged
        In moving order, all in all.

Yet what mean the stars in their courses,

THEY QUESTION
THE MEANING
OF EXISTENCE

        And the systems that rise and decay,
And the travail of infinite forces,
        And the sequence of night and of day,
        And the might of the space-piercing ray,
That flows from unquenchable sources
        And drives the thick darkness away?

Alas! that the meaning we know not
    Of star, and of force, and of light:
For the depths of the universe show not
    The secret unveiled to our sight.

THEY CONFESS
THEIR IGNORANCE
OF THE ANSWER

Though born in the dawn of all being,
    And sharing a part of all might,
And the whole of the universe seeing.
    Yet its meaning we cannot discern,
    Nor the secret of all things learn,
Some Power Unknown decreeing
    No lamp for us here to burn.

THEY PROCLAIM
THE ESSENTIAL
ILLUSORINESS
AND UNREALITY
OF MATERIAL
PHENOMENA

Oh mystery, oh mystery!
Oh universe, oh boundless sea
Of being, where as bubbles float
    All forms of matter through the void!
The planet and the wind-borne mote,
    The nebula and asteroid.
The stars and atoms come to be
    Like foam that crests the cosmic wave;
    Like foam, they are while tempests rave,
And are not, in tranquillity.

THEY RECOGNIZE
THE VISIBLE
STRUCTURES OF
MATTER AS
TRANSIENT
MODIFICATIONS
OF THE
UNDERLYING
CONTINUUM
BROUGHT ABOUT
BY ITS AGITATION

So, by the stress of cosmic storms,
    This bubble-universe is wrought
    To shapes with change and weakness fraught,
Unreal and unsubstantial forms.
Which, as the mystic ocean flows
    Of primal forces, something takes
And moulds to fabrics vague as those
    Which flame or cloud or whirlwind makes.

Matter is not the base of all,
　　Matter itself is but a guise
　　Of That from whence all things arise,
And back to which at last they fall.

Born in the primal stir of birth
　　Spirits of force and light and star,
We watched with joy the new-born earth
　　Fire-footed, speed its course afar.
We saw the whirling fire-mist form
　　A centre in its endless race,
And burst in raging vortex-storm,
　　And scatter suns and stars through space.

How soon the stars and planets lose
　　Their tresses of resplendent light!
How soon in darkness seem to fuse,
　　Dark masses, with the dark of night!
How soon their narrowing tracks converge
　　To that dark centre whence they came!
In one last dying clash to merge
　　In death and darkness all their frame.
But from this clash of dark, dead things,
　　Once more the glowing fire-mist breaks.
From which another system springs,
　　Another dawning cycle wakes.

On the wings of desire that bore me,
　　I soared through the regions of night.
The darkness was cloven before me,
　　Outstripping the speed of the light,
　　And the ages that flagged in my flight.
The aether was canopy o'er me,
　　Girt 'round by invisible might.

THEY REVIEW THE LIFE-HISTORY OF A PLANETARY SYSTEM

Unnumbered the planets arising
    I saw through the infinite sky,
By endless mutations disguising
    The being which binds far and nigh.

As the manifold Gods began reigning
    O'er the stars for a space ere they die,
And dubious empire gaining
    In an unknown, changeful clime.
    Nor else, in my journey sublime
I saw, save worlds waxing and waning,
    In a shoreless ocean of time.

Eternity, eternity,
How many names sprang forth from thee!
How many Gods, unseen, unknown,
    Once swayed the skies with boundless power!

But each was hurled from off his throne
    By one who held the seat an hour,
Ere he himself must vanquished be
    By other powers, who as days
    And nights must rule o'er trackless ways
In brief and troubled majesty.

What mighty Gods in ages past
    Held rule o'er this celestial frame!
    Oh who can name them, name by name?
Or who can know them, first and last?

As light of nebula to star,
    And star to darkness, and the dark
To light once more, such changes are
    The cycles of the Gods we mark.

So transient, insecure were those
    Ere Chaos hatched the Egg of Night,
    Ere Heaven and Earth, ere Dark and Light,
Ere Cronus and the Titans rose.

But spirits we of viewless power,
    Abide unchanged by changing doom.
And, as we wait the destined hour,
    Call to each other in the gloom.
We call in tones of trembling light;
    The aether bears our far-flung cries,
And, o'er the boundless sea of night,
    Deep unto echoing deep replies.

THEY, AS
PERSONIFICATIONS
OF THE
UNCHANGING
LAWS OF NATURE,
PROCLAIM THEIR
PERMANENCE,
COMPARED WITH
THE TRANSITORY
NATURE OF
PHENOMENA

The empty spaces fill with voice
    As spirit unto spirit calls,
And at our words the deeps rejoice
    Unto Creation's flaming walls.
We chase o'er heaven the flying years,
    We track the comets unafraid,
And guide the planets' rolling spheres
    Through the long tracts of light and shade.
And here, upon this barren height
    Rough scarred by forces of the prime,
We pause, to view with rising light,
    Another tragedy of time.
Alas, how like the rest we saw,
    For Gods are born as worlds arise,
And, by resistless cosmic law,
    Rule changing worlds in changing skies.

And like the worlds to death descend
    And like the worlds again are born,
    With birth and death as dusk and morn,
In rolling cycles without end.

Enter Prometheus

Prom.   Immortal powers, whose unwearied eyes
    Have watched the ceaseless changes of the worlds,
    I crave your counsel.

Chorus   In that voice we know
    Prometheus, wisest of the Titan race.
    Nor this the first time thou hast sought converse
    With elemental powers; yet what cause
    Leads now thy steps to this forsaken crag
    With ruin strewn by spirits of the fire
    And storms and earthquakes? Why at this dim hour
    Ere Dawn springs from the arms of dying Night
    Comest thou to us?

Prom.   There rests upon my soul
    The shadow of the darkness of a doom.

Chorus What doom can vex the deathless soul of Gods?

Prom.   The doom of misery deathless as their life.

Chorus Misery is the complement to life.

Prom.   Yet something worse my troubled soul foresees.

Chorus What woe is most foreshadowed to thy mind?

Prom.   I fear the sun of Cronus' power shall set.

Chorus That sun which rises, shall, at length, descend.

Prom.   Shall might of power pass like light of day?

Chorus Each ruler hath his fated hour of fall.

Prom.   When shall the hour of Cronus' fall draw near?

Chorus When one has strength to cast him from his throne.

Prom.   Doth such an one now live, and what his name?

Chorus Zeus lives, and waits, impatient for the blow.

Prom.	Zeus said'st thou, Cronus' secret son?
Chorus	The same;
	His hand e'en now yearns for the rod of power.
Prom.	Shall Zeus without a doubt seize Cronus' throne?
Chorus	Unless the spun thread shall be spun anew.
Prom.	What manner of God is this same Zeus to be?
Chorus	Stern, like his father, like his mother proud,
	Eager to grasp the power, and having grasped,
	Fearless to bend all creatures to his will.
	The sweet food of his hate shall be the groans
	Of enemies tormented, as he metes
	His justice by the measure of his will.
Prom.	How shall his kingdom treat the race of men?
Chorus	The race of men? What meanest thou by this?
Prom.	Know ye not man, the child of dust and light?
Chorus	We only know of beasts, and sprites, and Gods.
Prom.	Man hath been beast, is spirit, will be God.
Chorus	How can one creature have three kinds of life?
Prom.	The boundaries of his being are not fixed;
	He was most low, and yet shall be most high,
	Becoming ever what he wills to be.
Chorus	How came so strange a creature into life?
Prom.	When Being,* married by the kiss of Might,**
	Brought forth the first-born race of Titan powers,
	We shared among ourselves the empty earth,
	But everywhere beheld tumultuous stress—
	Blind forces yearning to the birth of life.
	Then said I to the earth: "Create and form
	Animate things from harmonizing strife,
	And ever changing, let the living flame
	Mount up through being's never-ending scale."

* The primordial passive principle.
** The primordial active principle.

At this I bade the warring atoms join,
And breathed a vital spirit in the mass.
Then the minutest beings sprang to life;
Alike in form and nature, but through strife
And changes from within they grew diverse,
And changing, formed new creatures. Thence ensued
Tumultuous life that swims, creeps, walks, and flies.
Gigantic creatures rose and walked the earth,
Then passed away. And sometime there appeared
The race of men, in whom the primal seed
Of latent Godhead, which with life I gave,
First sprang to flower, and within his soul
Man feels strange longings for the infinite.
For as a child long-sundered from its kin,
Yet longeth for the view of unknown faces
And sound of voices unremembered, heard
In dreams, so man, akin unto the Gods,
Yearns to the unknown powers of the sky:
The azure vault of day, the radiant stars
Of night, and all the awful, lovely things
That show unto his sight in earth or sky.
For in the varied forms of day and night,
Aspects of nature, whisperings of spirits
That dwell in field and woodland, or the vast
Ocean of waves or vaster sea of sky,
Whisperings heard only by the spirit's ear;
In things as these he seems to hear a voice
Familiar, heard before, he knows not where,
Which draws his soul to it, he knows not why.
For man in nature and the spirits thereof
Finds something near akin unto his soul
For which he longs, although he cannot guess
What thing he yearneth for, because his mind

Lacks understanding and the lamp of truth.
And in his soul, enkindled by the fire
Of high unfolding purposes divine,
Spring vague incomprehensible desires,
Because he is divine and knows it not.

Chorus Thy words are strange, much have we seen and heard;
But never have we known aught like to this.

Prom. Some truths there are, known to the Gods of earth,
Though unknown to the spirits of the skies.
Ye track the golden trail of flaming stars,
Stand in the void and watch the endless growth
Of planets, and the birth and death of suns.
We rule the teeming earth and all its store,
Preside o'er changing seasons and behold
The slow, sad climb of life through birth and death;
And mayhap learn some secrets of the dust
Unknown to your celestial sisterhood.
But put this by:—Since Cronus' reign must end,
And Zeus must wield the iron rod of power
With more than iron hand, shall I assume
At once the faction of the later Gods,
Or strive by counsel to resist their sway?

Chorus Thy counsel could avert the Titans' fall
Yet fate decrees it shall be given in vain.

Prom. Shall I then lend my counsel unto Zeus?

Chorus Zeus shall obtain his conquest by thy plan.

Prom. But what if I stand neuter to the fray,
Shall Zeus without my aid obtain his throne?

Chorus What fate decrees will be, and bear in mind
Zeus holds as foe whoever aids him not.

Prom. What counsel shall bring triumph and defeat?

Chorus How to control the power of the lightning.

Prom. What ye have said is as my own soul saw

Foreshadowed, yet one cloud of doubt remains:
I dread what fate o'erhangs the race of men.
But knowing not, ye cannot counsel here.

(Exit Prometheus: Scene gradually becomes lighter)

Chorus   See how the central orb of golden fire
Now sheds its effluence o'er this part of earth
As it swings from out the shadow of itself.
And kissing with its beams the clouds and mists
Transmutes them into opalescent veils,
And robes of sanguine flame and pearly light:
The gorgeous-hued attire of rising Morn.

Hail, shining sovereign of the skies!
    Whose might constrains the planets' spheres

THEY HAIL
THE RISING SUN

In measured tracks to set and rise,
    And mark in flaming curves the years.
Fountain of light and life eterne,
    Spreading thine influence afar,
Though countless suns in heaven burn,
    To earth thou art the central star.
Without thy light no life could be,
    Nor day from day be set apart,
The cosmic life and thought through thee
    That flows, we worship in our heart,
And hail with joy this rising day
    Which, ere the whirling earth turns 'round,
Shall see new lords extend their sway,
    Shall see another sovereign crowned.
What care we for the nights and days?
    What care we for the changing Gods?
We walk the heaven's trackless ways,
    Unchanged, untroubled by their rods.

A form approacheth from afar
    Along the rock-encumbered path;
White is his hair, his footsteps are
    Burdened with sorrow or with wrath.
Nearer he comes, his form is bent
    Unto the steepness of the way,
But in his visage thought is blent
    With majesty of mighty sway.
'Tis Cronus, see, he slowly fares
    Behind the mountain's dusky gloom,
Bowed down indeed, as though he bears
    The burden of impending doom.

THEY HERALD THE APPROACH OF CRONUS

Already the beams of the morning
    Clothe the hills with the glory of light.
With opaline splendours adorning
    The brow of yon dominant height;
But the ray, which that summit enkindles
    With the beauty of roses and fire,
Shows shadows of forms, as night dwindles:
    The Gods who aspire
To wrest from the hands of the Titans
    The sceptre of rule o'er the skies.
They have seized on the summit ere brightens
    The East with the beams that arise.
There Zeus sits enthronéd in power
    On a throne of the clouds and the light;
While his fellows, awaiting the hour
When the storm of the battle shall lour,
    Exult in their might.

THEY DESCRIBE THE HOST OF THE GODS

(Enter Cronus)

Chorus   Oh sire divine,
              What high design
Has to this crag-strewn summit led thy feet?

Cronus   Alas! I know
              A fate of woe:
Summon the Titans to this lofty seat.

Chorus   On the waves of light
                  Thy words take flight,
They shall pierce through the veils of the day and the night.
                  As force which controls
                  Each sphere as it rolls,
Thy mandate shall sway all subject souls.
                  On the beams of a star
                  We bear it afar,
It shall speed to the seats where the Titans are.

Ye Titans, lords of earth and sky,
        Whose rule the elements obey,
Hear him who sits enthroned on high,
        The sovereign of surpassing sway.
THEY BROADCAST   Where'er ye be in earth or air
THE SUMMONS   Or the wide ocean's vast profound,
OF CRONUS
TO THE TITANS   King Cronus bids you all repair
        To this high summit's council-ground—
Whether amid the fields of earth
        Ye watch the seasons as they roll,
And see, forth-cast through death and birth,
        The living fragments of the whole,
Or whether deep in ocean-caves
        Ye rest on coral couches cool,
Or walk the beach where breaking waves
        Cast seaweed in the tidal pool,

Or in the spacious realms of air
    Ye guide the raging tempest's might—
Attend this summons, hither fare
    On wings of wind, of cloud, or light!

Lo, as the tresses of the clouds
    Are shaken by the rising gale,
Drawn by our call, in eager crowds
    The Titans throng o'er hill and vale.
There, climbing o'er yon rocks, behold
    Crinus the strong and Themis grave,
And fair Mnemosyne and bold
    Iapetus, with him Atlas brave.
They come from the broad tracts of sky,
    From the wide ocean and the land;
From high and low, from far and nigh
    They gather at their king's command.

THEY DESCRIBE THE APPROACH OF THE TITAN HOST

Behold, in the distance advancing,
    With a glory far-spread from on high,
Drawn by might of four steeds lofty-prancing,
    Hyperion's car through the sky.
And there, up the mountain slow-faring,
    Oceanus, sea-lord, meets my sight;
With fair Tethys; and Coeus the daring,
    With Phoebe the bright.
Now more near on the pathway ascending,
    Rhea, queen of the heavens, I see,
Dione her footsteps attending,
    As due to her high majesty.
And Prometheus, the lofty fore-knower,
    With Asia the fair, meets mine eyes;
Prometheus, the clear-sighted sower
Of wisdom, the truthful-tongued shower
    Of counsels most wise.

On the mountain's side
The hosts abide
Of lesser Titans whom I did not name;
But to this height
Come those in might
The greatest, leaders most renowned in fame.

*(Enter Iapetus, Prometheus, Hyperion, and the
other Titans named by the chorus)*

Hyperion   As the flash of a ray
On the heavenly way
So swift came thy mandate, so swift I obey.

Prom.   As the lightning's flame
Shakes the heaven's frame,
Thy words were borne to me afar, and I came.

Both   Whatever demands
The deeds of our hands,
We wait on the word of our monarch's commands.

Cronus Ye Titan powers, brothers in command,
With whom I share the sceptre of the skies
And realms of earth and ocean, no light cause
Hath urged me to convene the Titan lords
In this most sacred senate of the Gods.
Ye know an ancient oracle foretold
My fall in words like these: "Thou wilt beget
A child, whose might will overcome thy might,
And cast thee from the splendour of thy throne."
Therefore, ye know, I swallowed mine own children.
But guileful Rhea, faithless to her lord,
When near to ope birth's portals unto Zeus,
Sought the dark caves of Ocean's sounding realm.

There, in her brother's kingdom, hid from sight,
Beneath the waves the pangs of childbirth smote her
And monsters bellowed lest her cries be heard.
There, where the green, moist, seaweed covers o'er
The pearly shell and where red corals rear
Their living branches through the tranquil tides,
Stretched on a bed of soft sea-moss she bore
The evil child, and with base guile a stone
Gave to her husband in his offspring's stead.
Me wretched! to put faith in woman's words.
Meanwhile the child waxed older and the wings
Of flying hours kept bearing to his hand
Their gifts of strength and wisdom, till at length
He sought our halls and claimed his kin to me.
I, as ye know, shared rule with him, but he,
Filled with his mother's guile, in an ill hour
By drugs o'ercame me that I yielded forth
His brothers and his sisters. From that day
I saw or heard no more of him or them
Till now they threat to seize my throne by arms.
For now full grown in insolence and strength,
They plot by force or guileful treachery
To wrest the rod of power from my hand.
E'en now they seized that summit where of old
We held our court with solemn rites of rule
And sober banquets worthy of high Gods.
There, where of yore was dedicate to joy,
And peaceful converse, and high majesty,
Resounds the din of arms and horrid jar
Of wrangling tongues in discord-breeding strife,
And counsel-darkening, peace-quelling debates,
Whereby they weigh what means may vanquish us.

And if we stay our hands, their lawless might
Will violate the sacred peace of heaven
And hurl us headlong from our lofty thrones.
This much of evil comes from Rhea's guile
And Oceanus' crime in aiding her.
But now if we would keep our seats of power,
We must debate how best to thwart our foes
And punish Rhea for her faithless fraud,
And Oceanus for the aid he bore,
And Zeus for his rebellion, and the rest
To cast from out the spaces of the light,
Through the wide void of ruin and the dark,
To gulfs of night and endless nothingness.

Hyperion   Methinks if we would overcome our foes,
We must prevent them in attack and seize
Their stronghold ere they turn to seizing ours.
So, while they triumph, little time remains
To mete out lengthy sentence, yet 'twere best
To drive Rhea and Oceanus forth
From this our council, lest disloyal minds
Bring ill to us, advantage to our foes.

Cronus   Rhea and Oceanus, get ye gone!
Leave these high summits and the lofty thrones
Of Titan powers!

       (To Rhea)

             E'en as thou sought'st the dark
To bear the child of doom, whose doom will be
His own undoing, get thee from this place
Unto the wide waste deserts of the night
Where darkness broods upon the shapeless void.

       (Exeunt Rhea and Oceanus)

But ye, the friends of Cronus, brother kings
Whose power is my power, and whose joy

Is one with mine, whose doom is in my doom:
Ye see how my rebellious offspring strive,
(Inspired by their mother's evil spirit),
To overthrow the kingdom of the skies.
And now I bid ye say what means were best
To turn from us the weight of threatened doom.

Hyperion   Let us surround the stronghold of our foes
And, by the strength of stalwart thews, tear up
The mountains by the roots, or they themselves
Hurl headlong through the darkness of the depths,
Ay, ay to fall, involved in burning fires,
Through endless tracts of unillumined space
To everlasting ruin.

Cronus   Oh Prometheus,
Thou hast been called the wisest of the Gods—
Nor deem I vain thy vaunt of sovereign mind.
Thou hast heard Hyperion's counsel—what is thine?

Prom.   Not by vain vaunt of all-surpassing thought,
Nor by desire to make my will prevail
O'er that of others, am I urged to say
That I esteem Hyperion's plan unwise.
Think not to overthrow by simple might
Him named by fate as mightier than thee.
For might of mind surpasseth might of arm,
Nor canst thou conquer craft by witless force.
Remember Zeus by subtlety hath gained
This much of power, and to conquer him
By means more subtle yet he must be snared.
Hear then my counsel: If thou lookest forth
Around this solid earth whereon we stand,
The air which folds about it like a veil
And clouds which float like islands in the sea—
They seem substantial, for the threads which weave

The warp and woof of being miss the sense
Even of Gods. Yet what seems firm and whole
Is but the aggregate of particles
Separate, distinct, and free to move about.
And these same particles themselves are formed
Of particles yet more minute, and these
Are structures framed of many smaller parts.
And in these smallest particles of all
Lies hid the key which shall unlock all might.
Yea, by the smallest and the least of things
We shall o'erthrow the greatest. Doubt me not.
For mighty forces lie asleep within
The forms of matter, and at times awake.
As, when the blasts of stormy winds roll up
The clouds, and hurl them mightily about,
The forces of their ultimate particles
Are set in motion and their influence
Grows stronger, till at length their might breaks forth,
And lightning leaps, blue-flaming, through the skies
And rives the tough heart of the knotted oak
And lays the towering pride of poplars low,
But strikes at random and without control.
Yet may the mind, by grasping hold of things,
Knowing their natures and the laws which bind
Their multitudinous motions, wield their might,
And the mind govern nature as a slave.
Thus counsel I by certain means to wield
The might of lightning, and as weapons hurl
Its trembling flames against the rebel Gods.

Cronus   Ha! once I thought thee wisest of the Gods,
But age, perchance, hath filched from thee thy wits.
What weapons need we save the naked might
Of our unconquered thews to smite and hurl

Those puny rebels whom thou callest Gods?
What need I do but stretch aloft this hand
To blast the world to chaos? Get thee hence,
Thou sickly babbler, shaming with thy tongue
The warlike council of the Titan powers.

Prom. Alas! with me thou losest thine own throne!

Cronus Begone! Vex us no more, we neither heed
Thy counsels nor thy threats. Thou hast disgraced
Thy sovereign by belittling his might.
And if thou goest not swiftly, this weak arm,
Whose might thou deem'st so feeble, may make plain
If it, forsooth, be feebler than thy skull.
And thou may'st prate of lightnings, and the might
Of particles minute, and whatso else
Of brain-sick fancies madness lends to folly.
Go, if thou wilt, to aid our foes, I need
No aid of thine, for e'en if all the Gods
Maddened like thee, deserted to our foes,
Alone I would defy with naked hands
Their utmost efforts of united power,
Certain to find in this my good right arm
A tenfold match for all their strength and craft.
But thou begone, ere violence cast thee forth.

Prom. If thou dost scorn my counsel, know for sure
The fates oppose thee and have fixed thy fall
Which I alone have power to avert.

Cronus Still lingerest thou, speaking disgraceful words?
Avaunt this instant, or, by mine own head
I swear, this hand uncurbed shall hurl thee down
To yonder gorge of ruinous rough rocks.
As for the Fates, I scorn them! What can Fate
Do or undo to check a free-born soul
Who bears his destiny in his own right hand?

But loiter thou no more, lest my pent wrath,
Confined too long, break forth, and I let fall
Unseemly violence on a kinsman's head.

Prom.   I go at thy command, in grief, not fear.

                    (*Exit Prometheus*)

Cronus   Thou venom-sting-tongued reptile!—Well, he is gone,
Nor is it meet I dog his steps with taunts.
But whoso of you here has mind to speak
A better counsel, let his thought be heard.

Iapetus   Our foes have seized the loftiest mountain top
And if we strive to storm it from below,
We fight at disadvantage, for our missiles
Aimed upward, lose their force, while theirs, hurled down,
Take added power from the steep descent.
Which to avert I counsel you to heap
Pelion on Ossa, that we may assail
Our foes on equal ground, and by the force
Of ponderous rocks, downcast them from their place
And crush with ruin to the nether depths.

Cronus   Thy counsel is right pleasing to my soul,
And well becomes our majesty and might.
This much at least is fixed beyond a doubt:
Our hands must firm the empire of our will.
And whatso lies within the bounds of strength
To do, that let us do with all our hearts.
Yet ah! the dismal shadow of dark doom
Clings to my soul, I fear despite my will
Our foes may triumph and our friends may fall.
But let us cast ill omens to the winds
And do what strength can do. Come, let us go.

                    (*Exeunt Omnes*)

Chorus   Oh what is the mystical might
        Which kindles the flame of life,
THE CHORUS
SPECULATES ON
THE ORIGIN OF
THE LIFE-FORCE And driveth through terror and night
        All creatures to labour and strife?
From whence did it first arise?
        In the flaming mists of the prime
Did it dwell, or the void of the skies
        Ere the dark beginnings of time?
In the multiform tumult of things,
        In the whirling cycles of change,
Who can trace its course to its springs
        Or follow the tracks of its range?
Oh what were the parents thereof,
        And how did it come to be?
As child of hatred or love
        Or of might in the earth or the sea?
Was it mind or force at the first
        Or blind chance with power as blind,
The bonds of the dark that burst
        And kindled the light of the mind?
And did life spring forth crowned and supreme
        As the manifest master of might?
Or weak as the strength of a dream,
        In strife with the forces of night,
Through travail and struggle at last
        Did it win its dubious way
To stand with its feet on the past
        And its face to the light of the day?
AND CONCLUDES
IT ORIGINATED
IN SOME
PRIMORDIAL
STRIFE OR
CONFLICT Yea, rather it seems that its birth
        Was from strife and the forces which drive
The myriad atoms of earth,
        And make all nature alive.

We, who have seen the world
    From the flaming nebula form,
When the burning planets were hurled
    Adrift on the tides of the storm,

THOUGH NATURE'S
FORCES HAVE
PRODUCED LIFE,
THEY DO NOT
COMPREHEND
THE PROCESS
Can we say for sure how the flame
    Of life was formed in the mass
Of matter congealed from the frame
    That was wrought with the years that pass?
Though we fashioned with turmoil of might
    And formed to the cosmic chime
The fabrics of force and of light
    Which we wove on the looms of time—
Though 'mid primal things we wrought
    With the might which constrains the skies,
Life passeth the reach of our thought
    As a mystery hid from our eyes.

THEY INQUIRE
AS TO THE CAUSE
OF CONFLICT,
AND IDENTIFY IT
WITH A WILL
TO POWER
Yet wherefore doth life from the first
    Compel all beings to strife,
    Of conquest as equal with life?
And e'en in Gods plant the thirst
'Tis the will to power which drives
    Each creature to yearn for might,
And urged by this it strives
    To conquer its rivals in fight.

THEY SEEK
THE SOURCE
OF WILL AND
INQUIRE AS TO
THE PRIMACY
OF MIND, FORCE,
AND WILL, AND
CONCLUDE THAT
THERE MUST
BE A STILL
MORE BASIC
CAUSATIVE AGENCY
Came this will from force or mind,
    Or from will the things that seem?
For chance and force are blind,
    And matter fades like a dream.
Nay, rather it seems that the will,
    And forces and all things of sight,
Are but shadows and shapes that fulfill
    A more transcendent might.

Behold! with measured tread the Titan host
    Approach the sides of yonder mountain height
THEY DESCRIBE
THE CONFLICT
AS SEEN
FROM AFAR   E'en as a mighty billow, foaming white,
Rolls with majestic slowness on the coast.
But as the wave, if some huge rock oppose,
    Breaks scatt'ring, roaring 'round its base,
So 'round the stronghold of their foes
    The Titans move with eager pace,
    Seeking some means to storm the place,
But looking upward, naught behold
    Save an impenetrable wall of clouds
    Which swiftly forming, in dark shadow shrouds
From every eye the Gods and their stronghold.
And dimly to our ears is borne
    Their shouting like the distant sound
Of thunder, or when rocks are torn
    By earthquakes 'neath the hollow ground.
Huge rocks they lift within their hands
    And hurl, but more we cannot see,
For the dim mists roll o'er the lands
    Down from the heights; and wild and free
The clouds are spreading, fast, more fast,
    And darkness like a veil is spread
By the loosed pinions of the blast,
    And shades like night on earth are shed.
As when the moon's dark orb obscures the ray
    Of heaven's fair light,
A sudden darkness spreads and changes day
    To instant night.

(Scene grows dark)

Just so a gathering mountain of dark clouds
    Spreads o'er the sky,
And in so deep a gloom the earth it shrouds
    As night were nigh.

(A sound like thunder is heard)

Hark! What can mean that distant rumbling sound?
    Could it be thunder? Yet I saw no flash—
    Or might it be an earthquake's distant crash?
Methought a trembling shook the solid ground.
Yet hark again, a dull continued roar
    Re-echoes, like the noise, it seems,
Of breaking waves that lash the shore.

(A flickering, purple light shines on the background)

And see the purple light that gleams
Behind the clouds, its quivering beams
Shed a strange lustre on the sky
    Which flashes like the lightning's flickering fire.
    Or like some fierce volcano whence aspire
Night-rending flames and burning smoke on high.

(Lightning is seen)

But now clear lightning-tongues forth dart,
    Their flashes like a sword of flame
Cleave the dun shades of night apart
    And rend the raiment of the same.
And now a storm-wind sweeps amain
    And hurls about in disarray
Dim mists and clouds of driving rain
    Along the heaven's wind-racked way.
And still the ragings of the blast
    Grow fiercer, wilder winds arise,
And terror, on their wings forth cast,
    Bears whirlwind banners through the skies.

While under foot the ground is rent and racked
    With earthquake shocks,
The mountains tremble, and in twain are cracked
    The hard, rough rocks.
And overhead the storm in fury dire
    Puts forth its might.
And lightnings pierce the gloom with tongues of fire
    And blinding light.

Still rages the furious fray.
    What hath chanced, who hath won?
Yet we know how endeth the day,
    Ere its light hath begun.
For the Titans must fall in the fight
Made blind by their thirst for might;
And the Gods must wear the victor's crown
And trample their opponents down.
And, as these lightnings pierce the gloom,
A flash across the night of doom
    Still points the way,
The victor and his prey must tread
To thrones of might or dooms of dread.
For, driven by the will to power,
Each creature triumphs in his hour
    Amid the dreadful fray.
But for each triumph one must fall,
Each treads in turn the way of all
    Like darkness and the day.

THEY SPECULATE AS TO THE ISSUE OF THE CONFLICT AND DECLARE IT IS ALREADY PREDETERMINED BY THE NATURE OF THE CONTENDING FORCES

(Scene becomes light)

But see, the veils of the dark
    Are drawn from the skies
And near on the mountain I mark
    A herald who flies,

Not the dark from the heaven so fast
  Gives place to the day,
As with wings like the wings of the blast,
  He speeds on his way.
The herald of fate hither fares,
  As passeth the gloom;
He comes, and the tidings he bears
  Are triumph and doom.

    (Enter messenger)

Chorus Lead.   What tidings bearest thou of the Titans' fray?
  Mess.   Cronus is overthrown, the Titan powers
       Are vanquished, and the rebels have prevailed.
       Zeus, with Prometheus' counsel, hath obtained
       By strength and craft the sceptre of the skies.
  Leader   How fell great Cronus and his mighty host?
       How did their foemen meet them, how o'erthrow?
  Mess.   Bold was our host, assured of victory,
       Although our foemen had already seized
       The loftiest height. Cronus, with fatal scorn
       Of craft, with vain reliance on his might,
       Bade his companions scale a neighbouring mount
       Fronting our foes, but the dense clouds and mists
       Concealed our foemen's stronghold from our sight.
       Then gave our leader orders to tear up
       The solid rocks by strength of stalwart thews,
       And pile huge Pelion upon Ossa's height,
       Rending the ribs of earth with mighty hands.
       Then from our new-piled summit we could scan
       Our foemen's fortress, strong it was and stern,
       Well walled with rocks upon the topmost crag
       Of the sheer mountain; but our foemen's selves

We could not see, nor knew we what they did.
And Cronus, thinking they had fled in fear,
Spake thus: "Those puny cowards, could they dare
To face the single terror of mine arm?
Much less, the might of all the Titan powers?
Fools, to put trust in strength of rock-built walls
Or height of lofty mountains to keep back
Us, whose least might could overturn the earth
E'en from its deep foundations, that could pluck
The sun from heaven and cast it through the void,
And fling the stars like pebbles, or seize hold
Of earth, sea, heaven between our brawny hands
And crush them into nothing. Know they not,
(Fools as they are) this hand can rend asunder
Them and their works, e'en as the strong, sharp tusks
Of the fierce-ravening forest boar tear up
A tender tree? On, Titans, to the fray!
Lift up yon lofty mountain of firm rock
And cast it in the gulf 'twixt us and them
To serve us for a bridge, then let us cross
And rend and hurl our foemen into naught."
No sooner said than done; Hyperion's arm
Helped by Iapetus and by Crinus strong,
Hurled the huge mountain in the vast abyss.
And, falling with a roar like myriad thunders,
It smote the earth which trembled as in fear.
Then leapt we o'er the bridge with mountainous rocks,
More huge by far than meteors which from heaven
Fall to the earth and trail the night with fire
Ere they fall hissing in the shuddering sea.
Or huger than the hugest blazing rocks
Which the volcanos of the prime forth cast
Bursting with roaring flame and lava-streams.

So huge the rocks the Titans hurled aloft
Against our foes, but they fell short, and ere
We could essay another throw, dark clouds
Rolled round their stronghold, and from cloud to cloud
Shot flames of lightning like a serpent's tongue,
And unremitting thunders rolled the while.
We trembled, all save Cronus, but he cried
In accents that would make the thunder dumb:
"Think ye we fear mere fires, like the beasts
That walk the forest's tangled solitudes?
Missiles more dread than lapping tongues of flame
Have we; as to your cost ye soon shall know."
But suddenly the lightnings, which at first
But flickered overhead, leapt forth and fell
Upon our host like arrows winged with fire,
Smiting the high heads of our mighty chiefs.
And whom they struck, strange trembling seized his limbs,
And his knees smote together, and he fell
From off the sharp ridge of the rugged rock
Into the fathomless abyss beneath.

Leader   But how did Cronus fall? For as I guess,
He fell not at the outset, but advanced
Even to the very stronghold of his foes.

Mess.   Thy surmise is correct, for although some
Fell, Cronus still defying all, pressed on,
And all the rest went with him, scorning peril.
We struggled up the steepy mountainside
Advancing inch by inch; our pathway led
O'er slippery rocks which loosened at our grasp;
The way grew steeper, and the lightning-flames
Kept striking one by one the Titans down,
While others lost their footing on the rocks.
And once our leader stumbled, slipped, but fell not,

Regained his footing, and resumed his way.
And so, at length, by much exceeding toil,
Toil that defies the power of speech to tell,
Our leader reached the summit with a few
Exhausted followers who could scarce sustain
Their limbs—the wretched relics of our host.
There saw we our foes face to face; they toiled
At something which I know not words to tell of.
Zeus foremost stood, commanding all the rest,
And at his side Prometheus, who, it seems,
Was counseling him how best to order things.
But when great Cronus saw the face of Zeus,
He first grew pale with fury, then the blood
Resurging, touched his forehead and his cheek
With the hot flame of anger; scarce the thought
Passes my brain so swiftly as he stooped,
And, wrenching loose the largest stone of all,
Ran forward, staggering underneath the load,
Aiming at Zeus the thunders of his wrath,
And flung his voice before him as he ran:
"Thou misbegotten reptile, viper-tongued,
Turning against thy father's rule thy hand,
And striving to o'erthrow by treacherous wiles
Thy Lord and thy Creator, learn by this
The author of thy life can blast it, too!"
With that he poised the rock to hurl, but from
The clouds that whirled above us and around,
More swift than thought a fearful torrent of fire
With a soul-chilling crashing downward shot
Full upon Cronus, and his nerves were loosed,
His knees gave way, and tottering backwards, he
Fell headlong, and the rock before him plunged,
Tearing amain down the deep-echoing cliff,

And striking flinty sparkles from the rock,
And smiting down his followers. But of him
We saw no more, for he fell wrapped in gloom.
Then sudden the clouds broke, and day returned,
But with returning light I saw him not.

Leader   But tell us, were there any who escaped
Save thee, and how didst thou escape the doom?

Mess.   All of the mightier Titans are o'erthrown
Save Oceanus, Rhea, and Prometheus;
The rest, we heard, are hurled in ruin down
To darksome depths of rayless Tartarus.
But as for us, I mean the lesser powers,
When Cronus was hurled headlong and the light
Of day returned, Zeus saw our broken band,
And, as I think, Prometheus counselled him
To spare us if we should embrace his cause.
Such terms were offered us, and since we knew
That Cronus' cause was lost past aid of ours,
We seized the proffered mercy, and were told
That whatsoever office we performed
For Cronus, we should do the same for Zeus.
And so Zeus bade me run before the rest
To see this seat be ready for his coming.

Leader   Dost know how came Prometheus unto Zeus?

Mess.   Aye, what I heard I can repeat, 'twas said:
Rhea and Oceanus driven forth
By Cronus, wandered thither and were hailed
By Zeus and were most royally received
And promised honours great in after time.
And when Prometheus in a little space,
Being likewise banished, came along the way,
Zeus sent them to invite him in like wise.
For he had pondered well that ancient saw:

"Whom Forethought shall befriend shall ever prosper."
And though Prometheus was exceeding loth,
He was persuaded, and went up to Zeus,
Who said: "Oh greatest of the Titan Powers,
Assist me with thy counsels, and I swear
Thou shalt stand forth conspicuous 'mongst the Gods,
Honoured above the rest in many ways."
To this the wise Prometheus made reply:
"On one condition only will I grant
My counsel's aid to further thy designs,
'Tis that the race of men continue free.
On all creation else I give thee leave
To work thy will, but o'er the soul of man
And mine own soul thou canst not dominate."
"Nay, were it e'en for beasts thou mad'st request,"
Zeus answered, "I would gladly grant thy wish."
Then spake Prometheus thus: "My soul misgives me;
Confirm it with an oath thou wilt not harm
The race of men." "E'en by my beard I swear
My hand will not molest the race of men."
"Then thou art made the ruler of the earth."
Thus swore great Zeus, Prometheus thus replied.
But what he further did, I do not know,
Save that they say it was his mind devised
The engines of our overthrow. But these
Are mysteries beyond my wits, and now,
My task performed, I must again return
To meet my lord and master on the way.

(Exit Messenger)

Chorus   Oh what changes of Gods have our eyes
                 Beheld through the years!
           One by one they fall and arise,
                 With triumph and tears.

Nor as Cronus was first to hold
    This seat of power,
But as manifold Gods of old

    Each in his hour
Ruled and were smitten, Zeus shall not retain
    His throne, but headlong hurled,
By one more mighty downward plunge amain
    Beyond the world.
For forces ever acting onward drive
    All things to strife or flight.
E'en the minutest atoms seem to strive
    Urged by the might
Of Love and Strife,* which rule the fray,
Possessing in alternate sway
The rule o'er things, as gladsome day
    And gloomy night.
And from the strife of atom-things,
Which force to endless motion brings,

Hurled here and there, to being springs
    All-radiant light.
But as from the multiform might
    Of atoms in strife,
The beauty of radiant light
    Is kindled to life,

Just so in the strife of the Gods,
    Their discords and jars,
When with thunder and storm for their rods
    They fight 'neath the stars,
Who knows from this tumultuous discord's strength
    What harmonies may rise,
From some calm vantage-ground beheld at length,
    Beyond the skies.

* Love and strife are the names given by Empedocles of Agrigentum
to the eternal cosmic principles of attraction and repulsion.

But see, the new-victorious lord of all
    Comes hither with his train,
Where Cronus held his council ere his fall
    To fix his reign.

    (Enter Zeus, Prometheus, and the other Gods)

We hail thee, Zeus. Oh may thy will
Be led by sacred wisdom still,
Nor turn aside, nor follow ill,
    That not in vain
Was striven strife that made thee king.
And may thy reign good fortune bring
To all, and to thee everything
    That thou wouldst fain.

Zeus   Now are we come to Cronus' council-seat.
    But who are these fair maidens, clothed about
    With star-enwoven robes, and their brows crowned
    With starlike splendour as a diadem?
    And what is their strange song, for at the first
    They seemed to threaten, and then blessed my reign?
Prom.   These are the spirits of the mighty powers
    That sway the worlds through the vast void of heaven.
    Prophetic wisdom issues from their lips;
    And their strange words have doubtless meaning clear,
    Did we construe them right.
Zeus   But put this by.
    For since success hath crowned our mighty deeds,
    And we have seized the lordship of the skies,
    There but remains to portion our domains.
    And since in this great conflict all our hands

And minds have wrought and laboured toward this end,
Now that good fortune, like the sun of heaven,
Gilds with fair beams and brightens all our lives,
'Tis fitting all should share in our great spoils.
First, and I think ye echo my designs,
Let great Prometheus choose what gift he will.
For 'tis to him, more than to all the rest,
We owe the happy issue of this strife.

Prom. Great Zeus, I thank thee for thus honouring me.
But what gift should I ask for? Some high throne,
Dowered with might and wide-extended sway?
Yet why should I desire pomp of power?
Can joy be felt in swaying others' wills?
'Tis vain; of happiness 'twould bring not more
But less, for all a God can wish have I:
Fair Asia's love, the joys of sovereign mind,
Whereby I rule as king the marshalled throngs
Of mighty thoughts that move the earth and sky.
And honour have I high 'mongst all the Gods.
What need I then of sceptres, seats of power,
And spacious worlds to tremble at my nod?
'Tis true one gift I crave, and that right much:
To have as my especial care the race
Of mortal men, direct their destinies,
And aid their first weak strivings with the might
Of heavenly inspiration, and behold
Their slow unfolding growth to higher things.

Zeus Thou hast thy wish, reign thou above the race
Of men and sway their fortunes as thou wilt.
But now to give the rest of our domains:—
Ye, Hades and Poseidon, are the next
In merit, and among you and myself
Shall the three realms of ocean, and the skies,

And the dark regions of the nether world,
Be portioned out by lot, and what each wins,
Shall be his portion to the end of time
To reign in as he listeth. Let each take
A lot, mark it, and cast into this urn;
And whoso's lot shall first of all leap forth,
Let him be lord of the unbounded air;
And he whose lot leaps forth the second time
Shall have the azure empire of the sea;
While he whose lot shall still be left behind
Shall have the dark realms underneath the ground,
With deep night as his kingdom, base his throne
On darkness, and compel with iron rod
The flying forms of fleeting phantoms frail,
The ghosts of beings dead or yet unborn.

(Zeus, Poseidon, and Hades cast lots into the urn;
Zeus hands it to Prometheus)

And thou, Prometheus, to whose mighty mind
We owe above all else our happy fate,
Take thou this urn and shake it fearlessly
And let the Gods accept what Chance decrees.

(Prometheus shakes the urn and the lot of Zeus leaps forth)

Prom.   Thou, Zeus, shalt be the sovereign of the skies.
Poseidon   Thou art in all things the most forunate.

(Prometheus shakes, the lot of Poseidon leaps forth)

Prom.   Poseidon, thine the empire of the seas,
             And Hades, thou shalt rule the realms of night.
Poseidon   Thanks be to Chance, who hath on me bestowed
             The better lot, and Hades, thou hast won
             The lot most suited to thy gloomy soul;

> For ever, as we walked the radiant tops
> Of the high mountain fastness, thou wast wont
> To wish for darkness and revile the day.
> And ever are thy thoughts in hue like night.
> Death and despair, ruin, much blood and tears,
> And sundering hearts that love are thy delight.
> Rule thou the dead amid congenial gloom.

Zeus   Taunt thou him not, for I am master here.

Poseidon   Thou master? Thou art sovereign of the skies,
> And I the ruler of the mighty main.
> How is it then thou claimest mastery?

Zeus   Doth not the moon's attraction sway the tides?
> And is not the moon in the skies? Yea, even
> This earth whereon we stand is but a planet
> With myriad myriad others hurled along
> Within the wide immeasurable space
> Of heaven, so I as lord of heaven am lord
> Of earth and all therein and all the seas
> And all above and all below the earth.

Poseidon   What! By some subtile trick wouldst thou be lord
> E'en of the Gods? What base new craft is this?
> Thou portionest amongst us the universe,
> And then thou mak'st thyself the lord of all!
> Had Chance given thee the ocean or dark hell,
> Thy craft had found a way to base on this
> A claim to hold the lordship of the rest.

Zeus   Think'st thou this earth is all that beareth life?

Poseidon   Yea, for what else might serve for such an end?

Zeus   What think'st thou is the purpose of the stars?

Poseidon   To portion times and seasons for the earth,
> To mark the quarters of the skies and shed
> Their influence that rules all living things.

Zeus   Prometheus, let him know the truth; say then

             If what I said was but a crafty trick
             To gain the throne of power o'er the Gods.
Prom.   This universe is not a system framed
             Around the earth as centre, but extends
             Forever, past the boldest flight of thought.
             And planets that shine fair across the skies
             Are, like the earth, spheres of firm land and seas;
             And some are filled with creatures, like the earth.
             The earth is but one planet which is whirled
             Around the sun, and all the myriad stars
             Themselves are suns with planets whirling 'round.
             So truly all things are a part of heaven,
             And Zeus, as lord of heaven, is lord of all.
Poseidon Thy craft hath made thee ruler of the skies.
             E'en so thy craft would cheat the Gods of heaven.
             Beware lest thy craft turn upon thyself,
             And over-cunning hurl thee from thy throne.
Zeus   Come, cease your wrangling; let us gaze upon
             The goodly prospect which our eyes can scan
             From this high mountain's point of vantage. See
             This measureless expanse of luminous azure,
             And those few clouds which slowly float along,
             Strayed remnants of the legions winged with fire,
             Which fought beside us with fierce storms and might
             Of heaven-sweeping whirlwinds, and thick dark.
             And there, behold the ocean, how its waves
             With multitudinous crests laugh in the light
             Of heaven and toss their snow-white manes of foam,
             And lash the shore with diamond-sparkling spray.
             Behold those verdant hillsides and tall trees
             Beneath whose cool shade in the heat of noon
             Might rest the wearied flocks and herds, and there
             The forest, with its many-whispering leaves,

Spreads a broad shade where wild beasts seek their prey.
And there, upon that mountain's rugged side,
Strewn with huge boulders and sharp flakes of flint,
Are caves where the swift-footed wolf might hide,
Or tawny lion, lordliest of the beasts
That range the rocks or desert solitudes.
And—
   But what creatures strange are these I see?
They walk erect like to the Gods, yet seem
No Gods but liker to the savage beasts.
For they are naked, save they gird their loins
With shaggy hides of forest beasts; some hold
Huge cudgels in their hands, and others bear
Long spears tipped with rough points of rude chipped flint.
What are they? Some base mockery devised
By the revengeful Titans, ere they fell,
That they might mock our form in bestial guise?

Prom. This is the race of man, which thou hast sworn
To keep exempt from tyranny, and which
Thou hast assigned to me, that I may guide
Their destinies and lead them as I will.

Zeus I like them not. They mar the face of earth.
For fields and trees and savage beasts are fair,
Being unlike to us; but these are like
Ourselves, and yet are like unto the beasts.
For they are hairy, with low brows, and love,
It seems, the dint of heavy cudgel-blows,
And strain of limbs in conflict, and fierce fights.
Yet do they walk erect and front the skies
With fearless gaze. I like them not; in such
Confusion strange of diverse qualities
Is much of evil. Them will I destroy,
And with my hands create another race

More to my mind, beings who shall not bend
To grovel with the beasts, nor threat the Gods
With rash presumption, but content to dwell
Upon this goodly earth in their own way,
Worshipping us with due humility,
Nor longing for things other than which are.
And them, Prometheus, shalt thou have to rule,
So thou shalt lose no honour by this change.
But as for these, let lightning smite them down,
E'en as it smote the Titans, or let floods,
Wide-wasting, spread and cover all the earth,
And sweep the hated race from out my sight.

Prom. In many ways thy counsel is unwise:
First, why wouldst thou destroy them? 'Tis forsooth
Because a few thou seest there appear
More like the beasts of earth than Gods of heaven.
But these few are not all the race of men.
A land there is by King Inacus ruled
Wherein men are not like the beasts, but live
As nobly as their wretched lot allows.
Judge not the whole by seeing but a part.
Second, thou wouldst create another race
More to thy liking, not like Gods or beasts,
And who shall serve thee, e'en as thou dost wish.
But two things are against thee: Canst thou hope
To equal in a day the slow result
Of Nature's myriad myriad rolling years?
And if thou could'st do this, 'twould nought avail,
For thou dost wish a race who shall remain
E'en as they are unchanging, and this thing
Can not be done, for Nature curbs thy will.
And though thou art the mightiest of the Gods,
Thou canst not bind the forces that impel

All Nature on the paths of endless change.
And so, even thy creatures must perforce
In time become quite other than they are,
As Nature, working in thy will's despite,
Would in due time evolve another race
Like to this race which thou wouldst fain destroy.
And mighty King, remember thine own oath.
Forbear to make thyself forsworn, for thou
Didst vow to yield their governance to my hand,
And not to harm them, so, break not thine oath.
But let thy word stand as a steadfast rock,
Man's safety, and thine ever-during glory.

Zeus   What! Wouldst thou counsel me, the lord of heaven?
Such boundless insolence deserves no word.
Yet since thou namest oaths, remember this:
'Twas by my beard I swore, and since my beard
Is subject to my hand;

(Strokes his beard)

oaths sworn by it
My hand may set aside, for never oath
Can greater be than that by which 'tis sworn.
And since, moreover, I did swear my hand
Should not molest the race of mortal men,
I shall reverse my doom and curse their lives:
So shall my lips destroy them, not my hand.
Let man be slave to multitudinous ills,
Let heat and cold, moist, dry, alike combine
To plague him, let the brood of fell disease,
Cold ague, burning fever, and sharp pains
Rack all his body, and within his breast,
Let grief, despair, fear, anger, hate, remorse,
Deceitful hope, and more deceitful faith,

Ingratitude, the pangs of trust betrayed,
Anguish of broken hearts, and bitter tears,
Tears that shall burn his soul as blood or fire,
Afflict him, let the substance of his life
Be one long yearning after empty things,
And let his wild, unsatisfied desires,
Feed on his heart and raven on his soul.
Forever let him struggle against all
The things which are, and ever strive in vain.
And whosoever of the race of Gods
Shall lend him any aid or ease his lot,
Let that same God, cut off from all the rest,
Be bound in fetters never to be loosed,
Upon the hard ridge of some rugged rock
Where lightnings, storms, and earthquakes, and the beak
Of heaven's wingéd bloodhound, prey on him.
And let the thoughts that pass within his mind
Be changed to wingéd serpents, venom-fanged,
To scourge with pain of unassuaged remorse
His soul who dares rebel against my will.
So, tortured by this curse, the race of men
May speedily seek respite in dark death,
And their weak ghosts my brother Hades rule.

Prom.   Great king, have mercy, let not thy dread curse
Lash with the serpent-scourge of threatened doom
Gods and mankind. Cross not the will of fate,
For fate decrees that man shall yet survive.
And hurl thyself not in the face of doom.

 Zeus   What care I for all this? Slave, darest thou
Oppose my will and brave the weight of doom
Which, by dread Styx, shall fall upon his soul
Who bends not to my will?

Prom.   I shall myself
Oppose thee in this thing, and whatso doom

Thy wrath may lay upon me I shall bear.
For what is fated yet must come to pass.
But still attend my counsel: 'Twas my plan
That placed thee on thy throne, and bear in mind,
The Titans scorned my counsel and they fell.
Thou wilt possess a more propitious rule
If thou dost still attend my words nor smite
The race of men with curses for a rod.
If not, swift ruin hurls thee from on high.

Zeus   Aye, do thy worst. I scorn thy words since I,
Firm seated on the throne of sovereign sway,
Obtained the reins of might and rod of rule.
And know that if thou floutest my will, my hand
Shall cast on thee a tenfold weight of doom,
And make thee as a byword of the Gods
For wretchedness and hopeless agony.

Prom.   I fear thee not. That which must be, shall be.
And time will show whose hand the Fates uphold.

(Exit Prometheus)

Chorus   Who first created the Fates and placed in their hands
    Rule o'er the Gods, and the sceptres and thrones of might?
For Fate is a lord above them, a power that stands,
    While the Gods arise, and rule, and are lost in night.
For when Being wove from the void the fabric of life,
    She gave unto all things gifts, as light to the star,
And life to the beast of the field, and the joys of strife,
    And change unto all things else both near and far.
But unto the Gods she gave as a gift of bane
    Grim fate, to curb their will and serve as a bar
To the hopes of their hearts, and make them strive in vain
    With an unknown Power. Nor can they see their way
Aright, although it seemeth to lie full plain
    To their eyes, but they strive and by shadows are led astray.

THE CHORUS
INQUIRES
INTO THE ORIGIN
OF FATE
TO WHICH,
IN THE HELLENIC
IDEOLOGY,
EVEN THE GODS
ARE SUBJECT

THEY PRAISE
THE ONE
WHO HAS
ATTAINED
THAT EQUANIMITY
WHICH RENDERS
HIM SUPERIOR
TO CHANCE AND
CIRCUMSTANCE

Oh happy is he who hath fixed his mind above chance!
    For he stands as a rock unmoved 'midst the tides of change.
And far below his feet he beholds advance
    Tumultuous floods of ruin in endless range.
But woe unto him who hath set his soul against fate,
    Though he seems to prosper awhile and to have his will;
For the lords of doom shall pursue with remorseless hate
    The wretch, and heap on his soul a burden of ill.
They shall make him drink to the dregs the cup of woe,
    And the days of his life with a nameless misery fill.
And drive him along the gloomy paths that go
    To ruin and death; if he would escape the wrath
Of the Fates, and how to avoid his doom would know,
    Let him turn not his feet aside from the righteous path.

Oh who shall contend with the Fates, or find
    Success in striving against their power?

THEY REFLECT
ON THE
INEVITABILITY
OF FATE AND
THE IMPOTENCE
OF THE GODS

Or who shall loose what their hands may bind,
    Or stay their seasons or fix their hour?
For the realms that to fate belong
    Are firm, and their throne secure,
And the laws of their rule are strong,
    And the might of their arm is sure.
But the might of the Gods is bootless,
    And empty the pomp of their reign,
And the hopes of their hearts are fruitless,
    And the strength of their hands is vain.
So they strive, and are crowned with a curse;
    They weave, and their web is undone.
They are fallen from better to worse,
    And they set like the setting sun.
For the warp and the woof of their days
    Are woven of sorrow and gloom;

And the ultimate end of their ways
    Is death, and darkness, and doom.

THEY ASK
WHAT POWER IS
ADEQUATE
TO CONTEND
WITH FATE,
AND CONCLUDE
IT IS ONLY
SELF-RELIANCE
Oh who hath might to match with fate,
    'Gainst it in strife to go?
Or boasts his wisdom is more great
    Than theirs, who all things know?
Although his strength surpassed the Gods,
    And wisdom great had he,
His strength would be as broken rods,
    As nought his wisdom be.
Though clothed with strength as with attire,
    And crowned with wisdom as a crown,
The Fates would smite with vengeance dire,
    And cast his strength and wisdom down.
However great his might of mind,
    However great his might of hand,
Against the Fates the one is blind,
    The other is as shifting sand.
Then let him not too much rejoice
    When triumph crowns the day,
Nor raise a vain complaining voice
    When evil is his way.
For good and evil every hour
Control the world with changing power;
And he who seems most blest at first,
    Oft must to bitter fortune bend.
And he who seems the most accurst,
    Is oft the happiest in the end.
In this lesson let him find
    Unmoved by circumstance to bide;
In his own heart, in his own mind,
    Doth lasting joy or grief reside.

THEY INQUIRE
AS TO THE
NATURE OF FATE

Then what is fate, and how arose
    The might which all obey?
Its reason and its source who knows,
    Or whereon rests its sway?
Is it, perhaps, as some have said,
    The rule of sisters three
Who sit alone, and spin the thread
    Of life for all that be?

REJECTING ALL
ANTHROPOMORPHIC
SYMBOLISM,
THEY FIND IT A
MANIFESTATION OF
CHANGELESS LAW,
NOT IMPOSED
FROM WITHOUT,
BUT INHERENT
IN THE NATURE
OF THINGS
THEMSELVES

But who hath seen the face of fate,
    Or who hath seen them spin their skeins?
And can a will, however great,
    Sway such uncircumscribed domains?
What then is fate? Some law eterne?
    Which guides the circling spheres,
And drives the planets as they turn,
    And labours through the years?
For what is greater than such laws?
    Can aught their might o'erthrow?
And bid the moving planet pause,
    Or bid the stream not flow?
Or bid rain fall from cloudless skies,
Or bid from naught a world arise?
For much the mind can do, yet still
    Some things in nowise can it change,
Nor nature suffers any will
    To flout its laws or fix their range.
And so resistless law appears
    The basis of this frame sublime:
In all the labours of the years,
    In all the mighty works of time.

By what means then, shall the Gods essay
    To fix their rule amid law's domain?
And how should their hands extend their sway,
    And how should their minds their ends attain?

Let caution still be their care,
  And let prudence encompass their might.
Let them smite not whom fate would spare,
  And spare not whom fate would smite.
Let them not from their pathway turn
  Through fear or the evils it brings,
And above all else let them learn
  The laws which control all things.

THEY FIND
THE SOLE SECRET
OF POWER AND
HAPPINESS IN
KNOWLEDGE OF,
AND OBEDIENCE TO,
UNIVERSAL LAW

For knowing the law that constraineth
  The multiform parts of the whole,
Is the only means that attaineth
  The might of the world's control.
And the one who on high would stand
  Must build on what lies below,
And the secret of sure command
  Is to dare, to will, and to know.

Enter Messenger

Mess. Hail Zeus, supreme of Gods, attend my words.
Zeus Hast thou then aught of moment to declare?
Mess. Prometheus hath given fire unto man.
Zeus Kratos and Bia, get ye straight to earth.
  Seek out Prometheus there, and bring him hither.
  And thou, meanwhile, relate what thou hast seen.

Exeunt Kratos and Bia

Mess. As I was wandering o'er the fields of earth,
  Mine eyes beheld a country differing far
  From this, for no tall mountains reared aloft
  Their heaven-piercing heads, as if to hail
  Those homeless wanderers of the sky, the clouds.
  But all the land was rolling, with small hills

And here and there a level plain adorned
With trees, and over all the ground was spread
The verdant mantle of the grass, nor was
The region desert. Flocks of bleating sheep
Grazed on the pasture; herds of lowing kine
Bent down their hornéd heads to crop the herb,
Or lay at ease beneath a shady tree
Chewing their cud. And men I also saw,
But, wonderful to tell, they did not wear
The hides of savage beasts, but were well clothed
In garments fashioned of the fleecy coats
Of the ewe's offspring. Nor did they obtain
Their food alone by hunting, for they had
Their herds, and certain herbs they also ate.
But some of them bore bows of cornel wood,
And well-plumed arrows tipped with flint or bone,
For they knew nought of metals. And they dwelt
In rudely fashioned huts of mud and thatch,
Or some of wood or stone more strongly built.
And one arose more stately than the rest,
With columns for its front, and as I thought
It must be here that King Inacus ruled.
But while I stood in wonder at these things
I saw Prometheus, bearing in his hand
A reed, and, coming to the palace gates,
He called for King Inacus, whom he hailed
In words like these: "I hail thee, noble king.
Thy prayer is granted by a God of heaven,
But not the one thou thinkest. Thou hast prayed
For what would most improve the lot of man;
And the Gods heard thee, but they heeded not,
For man they hate, and would destroy his race.
But one there is among the Gods of heaven

Who loves mankind, and aids man with his might.
And for man's sake he braves the weight of wrath
Which, well he knows, shall fall upon the head
Of him who thwarts the will of him who reigns.
But if thy soul be ripe for daring deeds,
And thy heart strong to bear the chance of woe,
Take what I offer, and this once possessed,
Not all the Gods have power to destroy
The race of man." Then followed much strange talk,
The which I understood not, but at length
Inacus ordered servants from his house
To do all things e'en as Prometheus bade.
At first they reared an altar on the ground
Of earth and stones. Then, as he bade them, sought
The woods, and thither brought the things he wished,
The which he bade them on the altar lay.
First in the pile they heaped dry leaves and twigs,
And cones, children of heaven-piercing pines,
And boughs, storm-wrestling arms of mighty trees,
Denuded of their leafy garniture.
Then stepped Prometheus to the pile, and took
The hollow reed, and placed it to his lips,
And breathed thereon, as one who would evoke
The hidden music of the shrill-toned flute.
But from the reed there issued curling smoke
And flames of fire which fed on the dry leaves,
And kindled all the pile to flame, and shed
Bright beams which seemed to emulate the sun;
And clouds of smoke arose which hid the sky
With shadow, pale half-brother to the night.
Then said he: "I, Prometheus, give you fire,
That ye may fall not by the hand of Zeus.
By this ye shall dispel the numbing cold,

And ague-bearing damps and gloomy dark.
By this ye shall reluctant metals tame
And fashion to your use, so that your hands
May slay the savage monsters of the wood,
And cleave the stubborn soil with metal plough.
By this all things ye fashion, all control.
Yea, and in after-times the might of fire
Shall drive the sailless ship through sundering seas,
Reckless of winds or tides; by this your cars
Shall bear you swifter than the flying gales.
Yes, ye shall even mount the winds and sail
The skies and chase the clouds borne by the might
Of fire-urged pinions; and by means of fire
Ye shall forge lightning, e'en as that of Zeus,
And make it serve your bidding like a slave,
And flash on lightning pinions o'er the world
Space-conquering thoughts, or dread destructive might.
Yet shall my gifts more foster than destroy,
And weld mankind in one by links of flame.
So shall the race of man approach the Gods,
And rule undoubted lords of space and time:
Lo! I have given man this by giving fire."
Much more he spake, but I stayed not to hear,
For when I knew the tenor of his words,
I left him where he stood and sought thee out
That thou mightest hear the tidings of his crime.
But see, thy servants bring the culprit here.

(Enter Kratos and Bia with Prometheus)

Kratos	Almighty Zeus, behold thy rebel slave!
Zeus	What word hast thou to plead in thy behalf?
Prom.	First let me hear the crime against me charged.

Zeus	Thou gavest sacred fire to mortal men,
	And scorned my sovereign will with impious words.
Prom.	And to this charge I render full assent,
	But tell me, what the blame therein can be?
Zeus	Slave! Is it not enough to slight my will?
Prom.	This hand hath placed thee on the seat of power.
Zeus	But seated now, I wield the rod of might.
Prom.	Power should ever be with mercy joined.
Zeus	What mercy can he claim who slights my will?
Prom.	Thy will sets not the bounds of right and wrong.
Zeus	But why didst thou give fire unto man?
Prom.	So that he might fulfill his destiny.
Zeus	What destiny hath he against my will?
Prom.	His being's nature doth control his fate.
Zeus	What cause is this that I should spare his life?
Prom.	'Twas not thy hand that fashioned forth his soul.
Zeus	What reason this that I should smite him not?
Prom.	Didst thou sit always on the throne of heaven?
Zeus	Not so, but what hath this to do with man?
Prom.	Dost think that thou wilt always hold this place?
Zeus	Yes, if thy treason overthrow me not.
Prom.	Fear not, no harm shall come to thee from this.
Zeus	But didst thou not give fire unto man?
Prom.	That did I, but what harm is it to thee?
Zeus	But is not fire parent to the lightning,
	And having that, will he not cast me down?
Prom.	Dread thou not this, for ages yet untold
	Shall pass ere man shall wield the lightning's power.
Zeus	Then till that time I hold my present throne.
Prom.	But shalt thou always wish no more than this?
Zeus	What could I wish, am I not lord of all?
Prom.	Have my words passed so quickly from thy mind?
	Did I not say this earth is but one star

That wanders through an endless universe,
Wherein this law stands fixed for all that live,
That being is a progress from the less
Unto the greater, from the circumscribed
To the unbounded, and all finite things,
Forever rising towards the infinite,
Have as their being's first and final law:
Growth without bound, becoming without end.

Zeus But if it ever be my fate to wish
For kingdoms greater than this earth affords,
Can I not leave this planet to its fate,
And seek what region in the universe
Pleases me most?

Prom.   But what if some fixed law
Was that no being could reach higher life
'Till something else had risen to its place?

Zeus Thy proof upon a supposition rests
Which may be true or false with equal ease.

Prom. More reason thou shouldst follow my advice:
For if this be untrue, 'twill harm thee not;
If true, thou wilt be better for my deed.
Yet oh, that all things were as sure as this!

Zeus I care not what thou sayest, I think it false.

Prom. Oh Zeus, hear reason, thou dost think thy rule
Is based upon thy will, that by thy will
Thou overthrewest thy father, and that will
Placed thee upon thy present seat of power;
So thine own will thou makest thine own law.
So far thou thinkest true, but ponder this:
What if thy will did but fulfill a law
Which rules not thee alone but man also;
And that same law constrainéd thee to rise
Above thy present station, and the race

Of mortal men become what thou art now?
And that the law, which driveth thee to will
For man's destruction, stands no whit less firm
That thou shouldst fail in this unjust attempt?
To speak more clearly, man fulfills a place
Which, in the scheme of things, cannot be void.
And since all nature, like an endless chain,
Hangs link on link in an unbroken scale,
One break would mean destruction to the whole.

Zeus   Pratest thou of law again? If there be truth
In thee and not loose babble of vain words,
Declare what is this law, which thou dost say
Extends such wide inevitable sway?

Prom.   That can I not, for when we speak of laws,
We mean that certain matters of perception
Present to us unvarying relations
To which we give a symbol and a name.

LAW IS
RECOGNIZED
IN INVARIANT
RELATIONS, BUT
THE REASON
FOR THIS
INVARIANCE IS,
IN GENERAL,
UNKNOWN

Well may we know the processes involved,
Whereby what we call cause is ever linked
To what we call effect; but deeper still,
Why anything displays the properties
Which we perceive in it or so affects us,
We know no reason, save that thus it is.
So, when our minds and senses feel about
This mystic frame of being, certain forms
Or forces stamp upon our sentient souls
Their signet and impression; and some facts
Arouse in us that concept we call law.
But why this is, or what is law itself,
We cannot comprehend; for our own minds
Deal but with concepts, images, and thoughts
Impressed upon them; but what stands without,
The author of our concepts, is beyond

Our power to conceive, for we conceive
But by its might, hence it we cannot grasp.

Zeus Thou speakest folly, waste no words on me,
But answer me these questions that I ask.

Prom. Ask as thou wilt, I still will answer thee.

Zeus Did I not curse whoso should aid mankind?

Prom. Yea, and thereby thou didst most foolishly.

Zeus Did I not threaten thee with direful doom?

Prom. Yea, that thou didst, and I did scorn thy threats.

Zeus Dost thou not justly merit punishment?

Prom. No just doom follows an unjust decree.

Zeus Just or unjust, my sentence thou shalt bear:
Hephaestus, forge of 'during adamant
Strong chains and fetters fit to bind a God.
Then take along with thee Bia and Kratos,
And this Prometheus. Seek the bleakest crag
Of Caucasus, where night winds coldest blow,
And where the full heat of the noonday sun
Beats fiercest, and bind down Prometheus there
With mighty fetters linked into the rock.
And, if he ever 'scapes from out thy bonds,
On thee will fall ten times the doom I mete
Now unto him. And thou, Prometheus, know
There shalt thou bide, exposed to heat and cold,
And mayhap keener torments, if my will
So urges me, until the end of time,
Or 'til it pleases me to set thee free.
But so much mercy overweighs my justice,
That even now I will reverse my doom
And pardon thee, if now thou bowest down
Before my throne, and beggest suppliant-wise
For my forgiveness, and dost further swear
By Styx itself forever to obey

My will in all things, and no more attempt
To aid again an object of my hate.

Prom.   Prepare thy bonds and fetters, for thou ne'er
Shalt force me to beg pardon at thy feet.
My body thou canst fetter, not my will.
And Zeus, once more, as ere we fought our fray
With Cronus, which was won through my advice,
I counsel thee. Thy threats of chains and torments
I hold in scorn, and thee I hate not, nay
I pity thee, for thou dost sow the seeds
Of future woes, and spurnest from thyself
His words who hath thy welfare most at heart.
So let not hate speak by my tongue, yet mark,
An thou dost as thou sayest, know full well
Thy days of rule are numbered: Like thy sire
'Tis fated that thou wilt beget a son
Mightier than thee, who shall usurp thy throne.
Now, if thy mind will hearken to the voice
Of reason, unto thee I will reveal
How to avoid this doom, but if thy will
Is set on evil, and thy soul on wrath,
E'en by that Law I swear, which ruleth all,
No word of counsel nor one servile prayer
For mercy shall thy tortures wring from me.
And as for man, his destiny is fixed
Beyond thy power to alter. Well I know
That fate is fate, and that fate must be borne;
And likewise that my bondage ends one day.
Now do I go, I pity thy rash mind.

Zeus   Thou overweening mocker, torments dire,
Bound with fell bonds beneath the open sky,
Mayhap will teach thy soul humility.
And thou, Hephaestus, see thy task be done.

And as for me, I seek the mountain height
Where we contended with the Titan powers;
And ye who have no task, come too with me.

(Exeunt Omnes)

Chorus Oh what is the spirit of man?
    Mysterious birth of the gloom,
With life as the breadth of a span

THEY CONTRAST THE INNATE HELPLESSNESS OF MAN

    He springs from a tomb to a tomb.
His life in the darkness arose,
    And in darkness he beareth his lot,
As a shadow that comes and goes
    With might as of things that are not.
And the days and the deeds of his life
    As the shade of a shadow they seem,
A phantom with phantoms at strife,
    And the empty dream of a dream.
For he toils, and as wages thereof
    Has death, and the dark of the years,
With terror and darkness above
    And beneath him travail and tears.
And hope that dwindles and dwindles
    As flame of a smouldering pyre.
But the light of his genius enkindles
    The night of his fate like a fire.

WITH THE SPLENDOUR OF HIS TECHNOLOGICAL ACHIEVEMENTS, MADE POSSIBLE BY THE FIRE GIVEN BY PROMETHEUS

Yea, the luminous ray of the mind
    Pierceth out through the dark of his lot.
What cares he though the future be blind
    And the empty past be forgot?
With the might of the flame in his hand
    And the will to surpass in his brain,
The strength of the night shall not stand
    Before him and its dark be in vain.

He shall mete out the world with his rod
    And make Nature bend to his will.
And the mountains shall bow at his nod
    And the streams his commands fulfill.
He shall make of the trackless waves
    A road like a broad highway,
And the forces of Nature like slaves
    Shall serve, and his mind obey.
He shall fashion him wings for his flight
    With flame for their sinews, and higher
Than eagle shall soar by the might
    Of his steed, whose breath is of fire.
He shall make a slave of the lightning
    And hurl on the thunder's wings
His words. And the dawn, new-brightening,
    The might and terror of things,
He shall hail as a part of his glory
    And claim as his right by birth,
While the skies resound with the story
    Of man, the master of earth.

ZEUS OLYMPIOS

A LYRICAL DRAMA

DRAMATIS PERSONAE

Zeus	*King of the Gods*
Ganymede	*Cupbearer of the Gods*
Pallas	*Goddess of Wisdom*
Apollo	*God of Light*
Hermes	*Messenger of the Gods*
Hades	*God of the Underworld*
Phantasmus	*A Shade*
Poseidon, Hephaestus and other Gods	
Chorus I	*The Muses*
Chorus II	*Spirits of Cosmic Forces*

Scene: The Council Hall of the Gods on Olympus.

The action commences in the morning.

Time: The Beginning of a Cycle.

ZEUS OLYMPIOS

(Zeus is discovered seated on his throne,
Ganymede is standing not far away)

Zeus   Come hither, my sweet Ganymede.
Gany.   My Lord!
Zeus   Why is thy countenance so sad today?
Gany.   I thought of the dark doom of sacred Troy,
And lovely Ida, where of yore I played
Ere thy great eagle bore me to thine halls.
For often had I looked, as day declined,
From heaven's high ramparts at the peaceful town
On which the last rays of the setting sun
Seemed lingering as in love; how little then
I dreamed that once those pillared roofs should fall
Amid red light, loud shouting and shrill wails.
And then, methought that nothing fair could last.
For are not brightest hours soonest o'er,
And doth not the bright sun his fairest light
Shed as he stoops above the western wave,
Ere he is hid behind the veils of Night?
So I did think, mayhap these golden roofs
And sapphire-splendid halls wherein we dwell
Sometime may be no more, and nothing stand
Save horrid darkness and pale shades of grief.
Zeus   Come, come, be merry, thou art but a child;
When thou hast lived as many years as I
Thou might'st then have some cause for gloomy thoughts.

(Zeus is silent a moment)

But go— See what detains the other Gods.

They should be here already, it is time
They should be here— Tell them I bid them come.

(Exit Ganymede)

Alas, what fear lies on this child of earth!
Too long the race of man hath suffered ill
To lose its sorrow even with the Gods!
And yet some sooth is in this Phrygian boy:
These weak, blind mortals have a subtile sense
Foreshadowing future woes, and all too sure
I see foreshadowed in my prescient soul
The gathering cloud of doom. Yet doom to what?
As for myself, I stand beyond the reach
Of chance or Fate, firm fixed in mine own might
On the eternal adamant of truth.
Then doom to what? Alas! unto the race
Of mortal men, who, in their madness hurl
Calamities on their own trembling heads,
Then blame the Gods for evils. Oft I think
How once to great Prometheus I did wrong
Because of mortal men. I knew them not,
Young as I was in power, blind with pride,
And drunken with the wine of victory.
Mad was I to reward with cruel bonds
Him who had been my best and wisest friend.
Yet do I blame him, that he never since
Forgave me, for when Herakles unbound
His fetters from the rock, I straightway bade
My lightning-footed herald to bear word
Of pardon and mine own heartfelt remorse.
Yet did he answer in an angry wise:
"Let Zeus not hope for counsels from my lips.
Once did he scorn my wisdom and bestow
As guerdon this bleak weatherbeaten crag,

This rugged bed of rocks, those galling chains.
Nay, if he crave my counsel, bear thou back
Short words but true: Through torments he hath taught
Me wisdom; would he learn, let him endure.
Who would be wise must suffer." From that hour
I heard his voice no more. Day after day
I bade my tempest-wingéd hound of thought
Search the wide waste of aether, but each eve
Amid the gathering shadows of the night,
With weary pinions came my eagle home
From fruitless quest. Iris I sent, and that
Bright spirit of light to whose all-seeing eyes
All earthly things are open, but no word
Hath any of Prometheus brought to me.
"Who would be wise must suffer." Thus he spake.
Have I not suffered? All the evil things
Which men have done, bring they not pain to me?
Do I not toil and struggle to advance
Their spirits on the pathway to the light?
Yet nowise can I lift their downcast eyes.
I sent them mighty sages, heavenly bards
Whose words were as a trumpet-call to truth
And yet, alas! unheeded by the ears
Of thoughtless men, who run their daily rounds
Of petty sorrows, joys, desires, and hopes,
Actions and thoughts, small virtues and small sins,
Without one care to pierce beyond the veil
Which shrouds in gloom their lifelong wanderings
From thoughtless childhood unto senseless age,
And—

(Re-enter Ganymede)

   Well, what hath detained the other Gods?
Gany. They hearkened unto tidings from the earth

And laughed that man, the sport of chance and fate,
Should so lift up his soul to vanity,
As doth a certain small self-righteous tribe,
Who hold in scorn the rest of humankind
Because they deem themselves the chosen race.
They have a book which says that God is One,
And therefore they hold all the Gods to scorn.
Well, Hermes brought us tidings of one man
Among them, who, he said, spent all his life
In doing deeds of mercy unto man.
For which the curses of his fellow men
Pursued him. All reviled him, save a few
Who called him The Anointed, Son of God.
But most called him blasphemer, hypocrite,
And mocker of religion: for the priests
Of that sole god they worship, gave commands
To have him seized and brought before a judge,
Who, swayed by the fell clamour of the mob,
Passed doom of death upon him, and the while
They cursed and mocked him, but in turn, he blessed
His mockers and begged pardon for his foes.
At this the heavenly Gods laughed long and loud.

Zeus But dost thou find therein at which to laugh?

Gany. Not so, my Lord, it grieves my heart to learn
That one who ever did the deeds of good,
Should have, at last, foul evil done to him.

Zeus Thou hast a tender heart, thou once drew breath
Upon the earth among thy fellow men,
And hast more pity for them than the Gods.
But as for me, I also pity him,
And if I could upset the fates of men,
Him would I succour, nor would leave undone
Aught in my power to turn aside his doom.

But Fate forbids. Ah, what shall Fate decree?
I cast mine inward eye upon the dark
Scroll of the future, but, alas, 'tis furled.
I know not what may be, Oh that I had
Prometheus here to counsel me aright!

(Enter the Gods and the Muses)

But no, it may not be. And see, the Gods
With solemn and majestic step draw near.
Here, in this azure-vaulted hall of state,
They take their golden thrones; alas, what sad
And hollow mockery of might are we!
Here sit we to debate the fate of worlds,
And yet not one of us can trace aright
His being's source, and Fate stands o'er us all.
Yet Fate hath placed us here, and we must act
Befitting this our station, and 'tis mine,
By ancient law and custom to preside
O'er this, the solemn senate of the Gods.

(The Gods take their seats, Zeus addresses them.)

Lords of the boundless sky, again the time
Returning brings us here to lay our plans,
And fix the laws which all things must obey.
And, as our ancient custom stands, let song
Begin our councils, to commemorate
How harmony, upon the mighty deep,
Made firm the first foundations of the world.

The Muses   Of the birth of the Earth and the Skies,
       And of Gods and men let us sing;
       Let our spirits soar on the wing
Of thought to where worlds arise.

THEY INQUIRE
AS TO THE
ORIGIN OF BEING

As the tone of the clear-voiced lyre
    Has birth in the stricken string,
As the light is born in the fire,
    From whence did Being spring?
For all things else arose
    From some prior thing,
But Being's birth who knows?
    For what could bring
Being to Being, that forever goes
    Unto the void behind
All things of thought, all vain illusive shows,
    All searchings of the mind?

In the dark of the birth of time,
    Where no ray of the mind can go,

THEY DESCRIBE
THE CONDITION
OF SPACE
PRIOR TO THE
BIRTH OF A
UNIVERSE

In the wastes of that ultimate clime,
    Was the primal ebb and flow.
For there, in the night of the ages,
    Ere worlds from the void rose to sight,
There was naught save Being, that wages
    A fruitless war with Might.
And the dark was more deep than the noon
    Of the darkest night upon earth,
When the shadows are thick, ere the moon
    From the womb of the dark has birth.
When the eyes of the heavens are blind,
    And the spirits of night seem to hark
To the moan of the desolate wind,
    And the trees that sigh through the dark.
Yet what ear in the cosmic night
    Could list to the dreary sigh,
As the winds of primal might
    Through the void of space went by?

When no sound of the spheral chime
    Nor any voice could be,
Save the moan of the waves of time
    On the shore of eternity.

But from the depths of utter nought
    A harmony, through all the skies,
The archetypes of being wrought,
    As seeds from which all worlds arise.
A primal power from the deep
    Called forth the basis of the world,

THEY DESCRIBE
THE PROCESS OF
COSMOGENESIS

And from unmanifested sleep,
    The seeds of life in darkness furled.
For through that darkness shining bright,
    With motion and with sound,
A ray of power pierced the night,
A portion of the infinite
    Filled the dead void around.
And, building up the cosmic frame,
Force vibrating to substance came;
    And life and thought through the blind mass
Were kindled as a kindled flame;
    And, as the rolling cycles pass,
Was wrought the raiment of the same.
Then Being turned no more to strife
    With Might amid the cosmic morn,
But from their union sprang to life
    The egg from whence the worlds are born.
The Egg of Night, through darkness hurled
    On tides of chaos, thence there came
The glories of the new-born world,
    Robed in a robe of starry flame.

For the primal motion played
    Through that mystic Egg of Night,
    And, as fruits of an infinite might,

THE UNIVERSE
TAKES FORM

The first of the atoms made.
Then the force which the atoms created
    Compelled their endless flight
To a point, and the mass gyrated,
    And a nebula rose to sight.
And as sparks thrown off from a fire
    Which burneth bright,
The stars, each clothed in attire
    Of gleaming light,
Came forth, as in that flaming whirlwind dire,
    Amid such mighty storms,
The Cosmic frame to higher heights and higher
    Must lift its varied forms.

In the forces that hurled to and fro
    The atom-sparks of the prime,
Did the Cosmic Energy show

ENERGY MANI-
FESTS AS FORM,
LIFE, AND DESIRE

    In the first dim dawn of time.
In the forms of the mineral masses,
    And in life of the tree and the flower,
Shone forth, as through all things it passes,
    The ray of its manifest power.
And its force, mounting higher and higher,
    Self-moved, as all being it drives,
Burst forth in the might of desire,
    That rules o'er the animal lives.
Then as first grey gleam of the morn
    That driveth the night from the skies,

MIND APPEARS
AND TAKES
COMMAND

'Midst the dark of desire was born
    Mind's light, that above it may rise.

But not in the struggle alone
    Could that light supernal have birth;
'Twas a ray of the infinite shown
    By its gleam on the forms of the earth,
Mirrored back by the souls of mankind,
    As the sun by the waves of the sea,
A flash of the Limitless Mind
    On the waves of humanity.

And so, from out the unknown dark,
    Creative energy was hurled;
The primal flame gave forth a spark
    Which formed the centre of the world.

COSMIC
UNFOLDMENT
IS LIKENED
UNTO A MUSICAL
SYMPHONY

And as a lyrist's skillful hand
    From out the lyre's sounding strings,
Their hidden music can command
    'Til all the air with rapture rings;
So the Creative Energy
    Called forth the atom-tones.
Their hidden potencies set free,
And wrought the cosmic harmony
    Through Being's inmost zones.
That endless symphony whose notes
Are planets, each vast world that floats
    Within the aether's sea of night,

THE INTERACTION
OF HARMONIC
PROCESSES
CONSTITUTES
THE MUSIC OF
THE SPHERES

Like the wind-borne and viewless motes,
    Is but a transient tone of light
That time to nothingness devotes.
Throughout the heavens near and far
    With harmony the planets roll,
For cycles of the systems are
    Harmonic cycles of the whole.
And so, in notes of boundless range,
    Resounds the Music of the Spheres,

As rolls the mighty Wheel of Change
    Through cycles of unmeasured years.

The world is one vast harmony
    Whose tones are atoms, souls, and stars;
Whose echoes thrill infinity,
    Whose endless being nothing bars.
Star yearns to star in cosmic love
    But cosmic strife dispels afar

DUALITY REIGNS   The shining orbs, and rules above
THROUGHOUT   The stable orbit of each star.
THE MANIFESTED   And as that dual might constrains
COSMOS   The planets in their tracks to roll,
A dual aspect all retains,
    And opposites the world control.
Spirit and matter, light and dark,
    Force, and the deathless light of mind,
These are the forms in which we mark
    The mighty Cause that lies behind.
As, driven by the cosmic storms,
    The atoms into worlds combine,
The spirits rise through matter's forms
    To glories of the heights divine.
All must approach a higher plane,
    Spirit and matter's forms likewise:
Through the long cycle's endless chain,
    To being's highest types shall rise.

Zeus   Gods of all regions of the earth and sky,
Enthronéd Powers, what seems of most weight
In the affairs of earth, let each declare
That we in council may debate thereon.

Apollo Much hath been sung of cosmic harmony;
And true it is, the atoms and the worlds
Revolve in measured cycles and display
Harmonious order, and in all the spheres,
Darkness and light, the seasons and the years
Proceed in fixéd sequence; all the stars
Resound the song of one harmonious whole.
But look upon mankind; through all the skies
Eternal order reigneth, but his deeds
Make a vast discord in the cosmic song.
For he respects not the high Law of Worlds;
And, giving rein to uncurbed lust and rage,
Makes for himself a boundless weight of woe.
For he is hurled about by fierce desires:
Like to a rudderless and oarless ship
Tossed here and there by passion's furious gales
Upon the trackless ocean of his life.
Either he frets at things he cannot change,
Or, coveting what other men possess,
Lays violent hands upon them, and destroys
His own peace and his fellows'. Then, mayhap
He fails in his attempt, and, brought to grief,
Blasphemes against the Gods, on whom he lays
The blame of his own folly; or perchance
He gains what he desires, but to find
The fruit of victory not worth the strife,
And, stung by disappointment and remorse,
He turns to struggle for some other prize,
Wasting his days in unavailing strife,
Losing his peace in never-ending wars,
Each man foe to his fellows. Oh great Zeus,
We call thee Wise, and Merciful, and Just:

But how can wisdom thus permit mankind,
The crown of earthly being, so to mar
The cosmic harmony with endless strife?
And how can mercy let him fall a prey
To lawless passions and unjust desires?
And how can justice suffer him to reap
The fruits of misery by others sown?

Pallas Yea, why is this injustice in the world?
The evil man sows crimes, and oftimes reaps
Wealth, honour, friends, while he who spends his days
In righteousness and service oftimes falls
A victim to that selfsame evil man.
And why is one man born to poverty,
With misery for his birthright, and grim want
And toil predestined as his lot in life,
Whereas another falls into the lap
Of luxury and wealth? And tell us why
Men are from birth unequally endowed
With strength and beauty, wit and skill, and why
Doth Happiness so seldom crown the head
Of him who merits most her precious boon?

Zeus Daughter, what word hath issued from thy lips?
Dost thou, forsooth, arraign the Powers Divine
Because of the unequal lot of man?
And thou, Apollo, thou didst likewise blame
The state of man, which thou didst liken to
A discord in the cosmic harmony.
Have ye not then some special case in mind?
Say what ye deem amiss, that I may show
However much seems wrong with things of earth,
That heavenly justice is not set aside.

Apollo Nay, an thou wilt, reply to my complaint,

	And then, if any case I have in mind
	Seems worthy special notice, it is time
	Then to consider special instances.
Pallas	My brother's words I echo, do thou treat
	The general first, and then particulars.
Zeus	I do consent to follow your requests,
	For, though 'tis harder to refute a charge
	In universals than particulars,
	I will essay to do as ye desire.
	For first ye say the universal law
	Is harmony, yet claim the strife of men
	Is not at one with that high law of worlds.
	Yet know ye not this strife is but a part
	Of that same cosmic harmony? Behold
	The creatures of the fields: the insects chirp
	Deep in the grass, the birds sing in the trees,
	The butterflies flit free from flower to flower,
	And all seems peace and joy; but is it so?
	Nay, it is war—cruel, relentless war,
	No quarter asked or given. For the bird
	Devours the insects that it finds about,
	Until the bird, perchance, a victim falls
	To some more mighty enemy, who may be
	Slain by the hand of man; and he, in turn,
	Bears arms against his fellows, till he falls
	Before the all-destroying arm of fate.
	Yet from this never-ending warfare waged
	By creature against creature, have emerged
	The beauties of the animate universe.
	The insects' gorgeous colours, the sweet songs
	And the gay plumage of the birds, the grace,
	The strength and swiftness of the quadrupeds,
	Woman's fair form, the stalwart frame of man,

And the surpassing glories of his mind,
All first arose as means to carry on
That struggle for existence shared by all,
In which the fittest forms alone survive.
Look through all worlds—what is the hidden source
Of cosmic harmony but ceaseless strife,
Strife so incessant and ubiquitous
That it appears like universal peace?
Think of the smallest atoms; hurled about
Hither and thither dart they, and collide
With one another, yet from such strife spring
The glories of the radiant orb of day.
Behold the planets, how their motion strives
To hurl them free through the vast void of space.
Another force strives with an equal might
To drag them to a centre. Yet these two
So balanced are, that from their endless strife
Come the majestic motions of the worlds.
So, from the strife of men there must arise
A glorious paean sounding through the years:
The song of progress unto higher planes,
The song of growth, of triumph o'er the things
Which drag him down, of conquest o'er himself
Which he alone through conflict can attain.
Next ye inveigh against his misery,
In that injustice seemeth to prevail
In his affairs, and that he enters life
Oftimes beneath the curse of adverse things.
Now to reply: as for his misery,
Man's lot was sorrow since the birth of time
Because he set his heart on transient things
Which pass away and leave him sorrowful,
Though the eternal lies within his grasp.

Did he but free himself from sensual lusts
And set his heart upon eternal truth,
Eternal bliss would be the lot of all.
And as for the viscissitudes of life,
These in the end he reaps as he hath sown.
Stern Nemesis, and just Adrastia,
And dread Erynnes, bloodhounds of the Law,
Pursue his steps and mete with faultless hand
The unremitted recompense for acts.
Man's spirit, whirled upon the wheel of birth
Through many incarnations, hath in each
The boon his former acts have merited.
This is why oft it seems that man hath not
The fate he merits; why he seems a prey
To others' guile, why he is oft undone
By his ill passions and unjust desires.
All these result from his own former acts.
And this too is the cause why men are born
With various endowments: some enjoy
The consequences of their righteous deeds,
And some receive the fruits of former sins
In adverse circumstances. In each case,
The agents that control man's fortune are
The seeds of actions sown in former lives.
So 'midst what seems unjust, it may be seen
The faultless Law of Justice rules his lot.

Pallas Well do we know that what thou say'st is true;
And yet, methinks, it answers not my charge.
Although 'tis true man reaps as he hath sown,
What if he knows it not? Can it be just
That man should suffer for his ignorance?
Oftimes he knows not of his former lives,
And keeps on heaping evils on his soul

Because he cannot see his way aright.
Can Justice doom a man to punishment
For doing deeds he knows not to be wrong?

Zeus   Thy plea is false, for do we hold it wrong
A man should suffer pain who touches fire,
Because, perchance, he knows not fire burns?
Should we decree that fire shall not burn,
Because some men through folly have been burnt?
Just so with actions: the wise man may shun
Unpleasant things by shunning evil acts,
The fool must learn by his own folly; pain
Alone can teach him to avoid the ways
Of wickedness and seek the righteous path.
So folly must be teacher to the fool
Who can learn only through experience.
Then thou didst say man cannot find the way
To act aright because of ignorance.
This is not so, for many have proclaimed
The path of righteous action. Many times
I sent forth mighty teachers to diffuse
The light of truth, and to point out to man
The ways of good and evil, yet how few
Of men attend the teachings of the truth.

Pallas Yea, it is here I find things most at fault.
Mankind rejects the truth, and he whose lips
Declare it unto men becomes the mark
At which they aim the arrows of their scorn
And bitter, deadly hatred. All too oft
The fruit of wisdom is the fruit of woe;
And he who loves men with a burning love
Must meet a burning hatred in his turn.
For dull are men, most loathe to change their ways,
And deeming wisest what most oft is said,

Reject the unfamiliar face of truth.
To such as these a wise man is a scourge
To goad them to endeavour. Welcome more
Unto the wearied slave the light of day
That doth but call him to unwelcome tasks,
Than is a sage to men. Behold the fates
That divers times have meted as their lots.
For some through scorn were driven to despair
And by despair to death,* and others were
Unjustly doomed to die as criminals.**
And others still the crimson-stainéd hand
Of murder slew.*** But all alike were doomed
To live and die in grief and wretchedness.
Where then is justice, when the sons of men
Must suffer for their ignorance, yet still
Reject the counsel that would guide them right?
In this threefold injustice I discern:
First unto men, who through their folly lose
The means of their advancement; second, to
The wise and holy sages, who receive
So ill a recompense for their good works;
And lastly to the Gods, who see mankind
Commit most evil acts and hold in scorn
The sages They themselves have sent, and hear
The heavenly music of harmonious spheres
Marred by the horrid din of human strife,
Yet find, in spite of all that They can do,
That They cannot improve man's wretched state.

Zeus Thou findest fault by viewing but a part.
And though thy words are true, they do but touch
A part of what is true: thou sayest mankind
Rejects the holy wisdom; but although

* Empedocles. ** Socrates. *** Pythagoras.

A portion of mankind still holds in scorn
That selfsame holy wisdom, 'tis not just
To lay on all the errors of a few.
And e'en those men who turned themselves at first
Against the holy teachings, shall in time
With or against their will be swayed by them.
As to the evil fate of those who bring
True wisdom to mankind, the one delight
Of the God-guided sage is to proclaim
The ways of wisdom to his fellow men,
And help them find the path of righteousness.
To such an one ignominy and scorn,
Yea, even death itself will seem as naught,
Because he seeks not praise or recompense
In earthly things, content to know his task
Is well performed, and trusting to the Gods.
And from the Gods he shall have his reward.
But when thou sayest the Gods can not improve
The lot of man, I know not what to think.
For have we not all striven through the years,
And thou thyself, great Pallas, most of all,
To help mankind advance to better things?
And what thou callest the horrid din of strife
Is, as I said before, a note which blends
Symphonious with the music of the spheres.
As thou thyself once thought'st when thou didst go
Triumphant, with unconquerable spear,
Amid the thickest strife of arméd men,
Rejoicing in the conflict that evoked
The noblest actions of heroic souls.
Why speakest thou not today as was thy wont?
Methinks some evil thing hath happed on earth
That thou and Phoebus raise complaining voice

	Against the state and governance of men.
Pallas	I spake because of what I saw on earth,
	The which, meseems, would show the present state
	Most evil, and foreshadow future times
	More evil than the present. For behold,
	My much-loved Athens is the Roman's slave,
	And everywhere the lights of Grecian thought
	Are fading fast. And can I not discern
	The gathering clouds of doom, which to my mind
	Foretell an age of darkness o'er the earth?
	Or, if not all the earth, at least the parts
	Where once our light shone clearest. For no more
	Do artists, poets, sages strive to show
	Divine ideals unto men; no more
	Doth Freedom hold aloft her sacred torch.
	Once praised I holy strife, when it in sooth
	Was waged for freedom, glory, and impelled
	Men to heroic actions, when it was
	A friend to progress, for in former times
	It was the best and noblest who prevailed.
	But now in strife I see naught worthy praise
	When it but means the triumph of the strong
	Over the helpless, and when those who should
	Remain firm friends become relentless foes.
	And lastly, I behold how holy men
	Scorned and dishonoured more than e'er before,
	Find all their labour for the truth in vain.
Apollo	Consider now that teacher who hath brought
	Glimpses of truth unto the human race—
	Truths which, to them, had ne'er before been known,
	Or else been long forgotten, or while known,
	Been by the crafty malice of the priests
	Perverted to false meanings. All his life

Showed love and mercy to his fellow men.
Yet what is his reward? He is denounced
As traitor and blasphemer, and condemned
This very day to die a traitor's death.
No more of him I know.

Zeus   First let us learn
His final fate. Go, Hermes, seek among
The realms of earth that teacher's prison house;
There watch whate'er occurs, and bear back word
What fate befalls that just and holy man
Unjustly doomed to death.

(Exit Hermes)

                                   What ye have said
About the present and the future time
Appearing fraught with evil, it is true;
Too well, alas, I know it. But the cause
Is not within our power to control.
For, as upon each day succeeds the night,
And winter follows autumn, even so
Amid the vaster changes of mankind,
Cycle succeeds on cycle, dark on light.
And now, alas, full clearly I behold
A darker cycle coming. Yet, ye Gods,
Be not dismayed, for light again shall rise.
The path of human progress winds about,
Advancing serpent-wise, seems to recede
At times, but still moves ever on and on
To greater heights, and at some future time
Shall reach a point undreamed of in the past.

Apollo But what will be the goal which thou dost say
The race of men in future times shall reach?
Whence did he come and whither doth he go?

Zeus   I know not whence he came nor what shall be
His final goal, no more than I can know
Whence came the Gods or what their final state
Will be. I do but know these human souls
Came to the earth and that they still go on
Through many transformations, among which
Man must advance through struggle, and in which
His sufferings are the ladder which he climbs
To higher realms of being. But the end,
If end indeed there be, of his advance
I do not know, save that I now recall
What great Prometheus said upon that day
When rage displaced my reason. He implied
That man's own destiny was the divine,
But how or when or wherefore I know not,
Unless 'tis that the noblest of his race,
The Heroes, Poets, Sages of all times,
Are types of what in some far distant age
The very least among mankind shall be.
For even now, some of the race of men
Have raised themselves as far above the rest,
As is a man above the beasts that creep.
Howe'er it be, it is to these the most
We look for his advancement, and although
Their lot seems ill, they have the Gods as friends.
So, let us now resound the praise of man.

The Muses   We sing the restless soul of man,
Inspired by Gods to toil and plan,

THEY PROCLAIM   That, through the sweat of hand and mind,
THE FREEDOM
OF THE   And in the stress and flame of strife,
HUMAN SPIRIT
      His spirit strength and growth may find,
And struggle to more lovely life.

Him shall the Gods protect, and lead
    According as he chooses right.
And every man shall have the meed
    That seems most precious in his sight.

MAN MAY
OBTAIN MANY
BLESSINGS

Blessed indeed is he
    To whom Apollo shows
        The gift of sacred song,
Or through the forest free
    With Artemis who goes
        Amid the hunter throng.
Or on the field of Ares gains
    The crown no coward wears,
Or from the Cyprian Queen obtains
In love a solace that remains
    His recompense for cares.
Or he whom Hera, Queen of Day,
Makes great with wide-extended sway.
  Or he whom Dionysos fires
With holy frenzy's mystic flame:
    The cup that ecstasy inspires
Is given him who seeks the same.
Or he who by Athene's grace
    May compass deeds of noble fame,
And, ere he ends his earthly race,
    See well-earned glory crown his name.

Yea, many blessings shall mankind
Seek, ere contentment it may find.
    The Gods, with still unstinting hand,
Shall unto each of men bestow
    Whatever gift he dare demand,
Whether his choice be wise or no.

But ah, if folly guide his choice,
    And, caring naught for false or true,

BUT THEY
ARE WORTHLESS
WITHOUT
WISDOM

He hearken to Desire's voice,
    What sorrows shall his steps pursue!
For every blessing fails,
    When folly sows the seeds
        With future evils fraught.
Naught unwise song avails
    To save him from his deeds,
        And skill in hunting naught.
Then crowns obtained through marital might
    In strife shall pass away.
And love shall seem a fleeting light
That gleams, like meteor in the night,
    Till darkness hide its ray.
And regal sway at length shall seem
The shadow of a vanished dream.
    And even ecstasy goes past
Like flash of lightning through the dark.
    So, if man wills his joy to last,
Let him seek wisdom's deathless spark.
Yea, let him of the Gods require
    Wisdom to guide each thought and deed.
And, placing mind above desire,
    He shall, at length, win wisdom's meed.

Blessed are those who seek for joy,
    But blessed in the highest height
Are those who for mankind employ
    Their utmost wisdom and their might.

THE GREAT
SOULS AMONG
MANKIND

The hero, poet, and the sage;
    These three are bearers of the light,
And guide mankind from age to age.

HEROES

We sing the heroes of all time:
Great Heracles, whose deeds sublime
  Made him as one with Gods on high.
And Perseus, who by Pallas' aid,
  Did acts by which he gained the sky.
Achilles, who so loved his friend
  That death he faced quite undismayed,
And won a fame that shall not end.
And Hector, too, his noble foe,
Who with a hero's soul could show
  A nobly gentle heart.
And great Leonidas, whose band
Did, keeping foemen from their land,
  A thousand times their part.

POETS

We sing of poets who have sung
With wisdom since the world was young,
  And taught the sacred truths to man:
Homer, who showed the human soul
With verse in sound like ocean's roll,
  And vast as all the worlds in plan.
And Hesiod, whose humbler lays
Scorned not to tell of Works and Days,
  Yet dared of Gods to sing the birth.
And Pindar's eagle-flights of song,
And Aeschylus, whose genius strong
  Portrayed the heavenly Gods on earth.
And those two Romans of great fame—
  Virgil, who followed Homer's flight,
  Lucretius, who loved wisdom's light,
Yet lost it amid matter's frame.

SAGES

We sing the sages of the past:
Pythagoras, whose mind amassed

The wealth of number's mystic law.
And Heraclitus' thought profound,
    Who first the flux of being saw,
    With atoms moving to and fro.
The flow amid the fixed he found,
    And fixity amid the flow.
And others too, of high renown—
Socrates, crowned with wisdom's crown,
    And Plato the divine,
Whose mighty genius toiled to rear
A beacon above hope and fear,
    Whereon truth's light could shine.
Much praise we these, the kings of thought,
But also those who ever sought
    Through nature nature's law to learn.
Great Archimedes, who first weighed
All things in water, and who made
    Rome's ships with focused sunlight burn.
And Heron, who with skillful hand
More subtile forces could command,
    And govern substances more rare.
The force of steam he first could wield
And to his will compelled to yield
    The power of imprisoned air.
And those we sing, as yet unknown,
    Whose hands shall grasp the lightning's power,
    And man with strength and wisdom dower
To hurl foul error from its throne.

ARE THE GUIDES
OF HUMANITY

Great spirits, worthy to be sung
    By Gods of heaven, their high fame
Is past the praise of any tongue,
    And the clear glory of their name
Shall men across the ages find

Writ o'er the years in words of flame
As beacon lights to guide mankind.

Pallas   Well is it for the Gods to sing the praise
Of wisdom and the sages of mankind.
Yet better would it be should they debate
How best to aid mankind. For while we speak
We do but scatter idle words; the time
Is surely come for action; for we see
Millions of hands, all reaching out, for what?
Millions of minds all searching in the dark
And yet, what seek they? This, alas, they know not.
They yearn for wisdom, happiness, and power,
Yet know not where to find them. And meanwhile
The strong oppress the weak, and those most bold
Strive to induce the rest to follow them,
And lead them into sorrow and despair.
A thousand warring creeds distract their minds,
A thousand warring tongues confuse their thought,
A thousand warring tribes contend against
Each other. And how then can any man
Find joy or blessedness amid this jar?

Zeus   As things are now, so have they ever been;
And if we hope to help in future times,
We cannot deal in generalities.
So, if we wish to better things of earth,
Let us hear one by one the things amiss,
And in each case debate what may be done.

Pallas   'Twas I who raised objections to the state
Of things as they are now, and therefore I
Will first relate what seems the most amiss.
'Tis that the nation that best fitted seemed
To bear the torch of wisdom for mankind,

Should fall a prey unto intestine strife,
And then, to foreign power. It was not
The Roman sword that made the Greeks its prey.
For, had they but kept peace among themselves,
They could have smitten Romans as they smote
The Persians on the fields of Marathon,
Thermopylae, and on the wind-ploughed bay
Of seat-girt Salamis. But ah! alas!
When Athens against Sparta raised her hand
In curséd strife, the doom of Greece was sealed.
How hard we strove to stay that fatal strife,
And to pursuade Athenians to pursue
A saner course, and follow wisdom's ways.
But siren-songs of glory and of might
Rang in their ears, and fatal love of gold
Made blind their eyes to see the woes ahead.
So Athens fell and with her all the light
Of Hellas. Then swift woes on woes succeed.
For soon her conquerors themselves must reap
The fruits their deeds have sown, when the strong hand
Of Macedonia rises to subdue
The iron rule of Sparta. Then once more
Did Athens suffer conquest; all in vain
Her mightiest orator oft raised his voice
Against the Macedonians' rising power.
Yet we permitted Alexander's deeds,
Since, by his widespread conquests he diffused
The light of Grecian culture o'er the world,
And founded that new city of his name
On Egypt's shore, where now great wisdom's light
More brightly burns than elsewhere. On his death
His empire fell to fragments. But meanwhile
The Romans, men of iron and of blood,

Laid low their ancient enemies and sought
For greater conquests. Then, indeed, Greece fell.
But we could not avert that final strife
Although its issue grieved us sore; we knew
'Twas but the Nemesis which followed deeds
The Greeks themselves had done when they gave way
To mutual hatred and to civil strife.
But then, alas, the Romans have done deeds
Far worse than any that the Greeks had done.
For most of them are cruel; war they love,
And bloody spectacles are their delight.
'Tis true they had some virtues; they were brave
And faithful in their love for hearth and home,
And constant in the worship of the Gods.
Well skilled were they in law and government,
And arts of war, well fitted to impose
Upon a conquered world the peace of arms.
But judged beside the Greeks they seemed scarce more
Than rude barbarians. They had no art
Or culture then, and what they since acquired
They learned from those they conquered. But they lost
Their ancient virtues, and from day to day
Sank deeper into vice. First, in the flames
Of civil strife their freedom was destroyed;
Then luxury and license sowed the seeds
Of total ruin; until now we see
Rome tremble 'neath a coward tyrant's hand.
And what more ills the future hath in store
I can but guess. But to my mind it seems
That Rome in turn will fall before the power
Of nations still more barbarous. And then,
Oh where will wisdom dwell among mankind?
My mind foresees dark ages yet to come.

For still, alas, more clearly it appears
That Greece, Rome, Egypt, all the ancient world,
Sink deeper into ruin. Oh great Zeus,
What cause can underlie these diverse ills,
And by what ways, if e'en by any way,
May we avert the evils yet to come?

Zeus Thou wert most near the truth when thou didst say
That evils are the fruit of evil deeds.
For with each of the nations thou hast named
'Twas their own vices wrought their overthrow;
And lust of conquest ever shall bring down
Conquest upon the conqueror. Hope of power
Led them astray, as oft it leads mankind,
When, not content with what the Gods bestow,
Man lusts for boundless might. So fell Chaldea,
So Persia, Athens, Sparta, Macedon;
And so shall every race in future times,
Which seeks to rule the world. This is the law
Which governs all man's actions and compels
Him in all things to reap as he hath sown.
And this law stands immutable as that
Which binds the planets to their measured tracks.
So, neither men nor nations can escape
In any wise the fruits of their own deeds.
And, though it seem an evil thing to thee
That nations, once renowned through all the earth
For learning and for power, should decline
And fall a prey unto less noble hands,
This too fulfills the law. For never cause
Is set in motion but it must produce
Its due effect, so never an effect
Can be without its cause. No earthly thing
Could e'er exist and fail to be the cause

Of vast effects throughout the whole of time.
No flame has ever burned that did not send
Swift light-waves flashing ever on and on
Beyond the farthest star of all the skies,
On through the boundless caverns of the dim
Infinities and dread eternities.
So are the works of men: their forms of law,
Their customs, institutions, nations, races,
Are transient causes which perform their parts,
Then pass away, e'en as a flame is quenched;
But the effects they kindle shall not pass.
For the vast world is nothing but a school
In which all living things at length must learn
Eternal wisdom. Nations of all times,
With all their strange viscissitudes, are but
The classes wherein human souls are taught
The lessons of the ages, and attain
At length to perfect wisdom. For the end
Of nature is advancement, and in chief,
Man, as the highest flower of earthly life,
Must rise unto the perfect light of truth.

Pallas But wherefore, if 'tis true as thou hast said
That all things must advance, doth it befall
That nations do not steadily progress,
But rise to power, then fall into decay?
If all the worlds are bound by causal law,
Why is it that the nations through which men
May rise unto perfection do not rise
In an unbroken progress, but instead
So oft succumb to ruin and decay?
And lastly, how can it fulfill the law
When nations turn from virtue unto vice?

Zeus In this respect are nations not alone.

For in all nature the particular
Is subject still to growth and to decline,
Whereas the general shows eternal growth.
Behold the bodies of all living souls:
They are born, they grow, mature, wax old, and die;
Whereas the souls within them ever grow
To greater strength and wisdom. Such the fate
Of nations and of races; they arise,
Wax great in power, yearn for wide renown,
And presently decline again to naught.
But through this endless change the human soul
Gains to itself the fruit of many lives,
And mounts to wisdom. All things of the world,
Bound by the laws of matter, are compelled
To pass through birth, growth, strength, decline, and death.
E'en as each human spirit must assume
A carnal body, and while in the flesh,
Be subject to the laws which rule that state,
Just so ideals embody in the forms
Of races, nations, institutions, which
Are ruled by that same law of birth and death.
But then another and especial cause
Of the existing evils is that law
Of cycles, which on smaller scale we see
Reflected in the cycles of the stars,
The cycles in the changes of all worlds,
The cycles in all motion. And in this,
The present age, mankind hath entered on
A cycle of decline wherein the souls
Returning to the earth are less mature
Than their forerunners. Hence it is men seem
Sinking to vices, for the hosts of souls
That now return to be reborn as men

Have not yet learned to lead a nobler life.
And lower things must sink, yea, until all
The nations which seemed greatest in the past,
Shall all but pass away, and the world seem
Relapsing into savagery; but still
When it hath reached the lowest state of all,
'Twill rise again, and in the future time
Shall nations rise more mighty than of old,
And all the glories of the storied past
Shall be once more enacted. But meanwhile
The light of wisdom of the ancient world
Shall not have wholly perished from the earth.
For some shall sleep in records, and some parts
Of earth shall not be touched by such decay,
But stand amid the gloom of ignorance
As a lone pharos through a night of storm.

Pallas   Thou sayest the purpose of all earthly things
Is the advancement of the human soul.
But how accords it with this scheme of things
That men are taught false doctrines? It would seem
That they could best be aided by the truth.
For some relate strange fables of the Gods:
Even among the wisest of mankind,
Our names are oftimes slandered in feigned tales,
So that our mighty Plato was displeased
With poets for the fables they had told
Of the high Gods. And others, less advanced,
Conceive the Gods as monsters full of hate,
Which they would fain appease with savage rites
Of flame, and blood, and human sacrifice.
In their bewildered groping, men know not
The nature of the Gods, nor do they know
E'en what they are themselves, they are misled

By ignorance, and wander without light
Through endless mazes of confuséd thought.

Zeus 'Tis true that many false ideas are rife
Within the minds of men, and yet they have
As much of truth as their own minds can grasp.
And as for fables of the Gods, ye know
That as one blind from birth can sense no light,
So most of men, blind unto things divine,
Know naught of that quintessence of pure light
Wherein the Truth has being, and to such
Must allegory show in fancy's shapes,
Broken and stained reflections of High Truths,
Ineffable in language of the earth.
And yet, despite their errors, they are not
So far removed from truth. What though they call
To us amid strange rites, by uncouth names,
If they but own existence of some powers
Of justice in the world? But as for those
Who think to please the Gods by cruelty,
Their gods are shadows, cast by their own souls
Upon the face of Nature. As man is,
So doth he hold the things unknown to be.
And he, by much experience, must learn
The error of his ways, and to discern
The sharp distinction between Good and Ill.
For not one being throughout all the worlds,
Hath power to change another being's mind
Against its will, and there is this of right
In this the present order, since not one
Of all the beings in the universe
Can blame another for its evil state.

Pallas 'Tis true that men by varied names invoke
The Gods of heaven, and have varied terms

For their own concepts of Divinity.
The Jews adore Jehovah, and regard
The other Gods as but His messengers.*
The wise Egyptians call on Ammon Ra;
The Hindus worship Brahma, Vishnu, Shiva;
While Persians, whom great Zarathustra taught,
Invoke Ahura Mazda, Lord of Light;
And the wild tribes beneath the northern sky,
Revere great Odin, wisest of the Gods.
But what avail mere names, and what though men
Adore the Powers of Justice in the sky,
If their own actions be not just on earth?
And what though men may worship Powers Divine,
If yet they know not what they are themselves,
Much less the proper essence of the Gods?

Zeus   Thy words of many answers would admit;
But see—What forms approach this sacred height.
They are the same as I beheld that day
When, having conquered Cronus, I possessed
For the first time the kingdom of the skies.
Mayhap they come to show some dire event
Which now the pregnant hour may bring forth.
Nearer they come, and hark, what words they say:

(Enter the Spirits of Cosmic Forces)

The Spirits   Thou hast bound as the band of thy brow,
                   Change and the sorrow thereof:
THE PERSONIFIED   For a darkness that hung above
LAWS OF NATURE   Shall come to thee now.
WARN THE GODS
OF THE IMPEND-   From the earth shall come forth sorrows
ING DOOM   To make the high Gods bow.
                   And the terrors of grievous morrows
                  The lords of earth shall cow.

* Angels: from *angelloi,* meaning messengers.

Yea, change is a grievous thing
    And its fruit is bitter with tears,
And swift is its flight on the wing
    Of time through the limitless years.
For, as waves of the sea never ceasing,
    Encroach on the storm-beaten shore,
And anon, their strength decreasing,
Ebb off, the land releasing,
    Even so, evermore,
The waves of an infinite ocean
    Rise up on an ultimate strand,
Then ebb, and sweep off in their motion
    All things from the land.

CHANGE IS
UNIVERSAL AND
INEVITABLE,
THE WORLD,
A FLEETING
APPARITION

For naught shall unchanged abide:
    Not the warp and the woof of the skies,
    Not the planets that set and that rise,
And the ages divide.
    For the Cosmos came into being
With change on every side,
    From a source beyond thought or seeing,
That veils of darkness hide.
While the forms of the stars and the sun
    From flames of the nebulae came,
And anon, when their cycle is run,
    Return unto nebulous flame.
For the world of our error-bound dreaming,
    Is the shadow an infinite light
Casts forth, for a moment, in seeming,
As a lightning flash, bright-gleaming,
    Illumines the night.

And as flash through the darkness swift-darting,
    The forms of the visible world
For a moment appear, and, departing,
    To chaos are hurled.

What is the world? A gleam of fire
Whose flames, ne'er pausing, ever mounting higher,
    Appear in changing forms.
And, driven as by ragings of desire,
    Mix in the cosmic storms.
And what is change? A veil of darkness woven
    Upon the looms of ever-moving might,
That weave illusions, scarcely to be cloven
    By thought, far-piercing through deceiving night.
And what are ye, amid these shadows bearing
    Aspects unmoved, more steadfast than a star?
For, though ye seem above the need of caring,
    Ye know not what ye are.
While time, with swift and noiseless wings,
    Sweeps through all regions near and far,
And acts on all existing things
    With mighty force to make or mar.
And though the Gods are great in might,
    Here shall their power naught avail:
With time in its resistless flight,
    O'er them at length shall change prevail.

THE
UNIVERSALITY
OF CYCLIC
PROCESSES

But amid all these manifold changes,
    One law with an infinite sway,
All things in due order arranges,
    And fixes the times of their stay.
'Tis that all things in order proceeding
    Must the cyclic law obey,

With cycle on cycle succeeding
    As night succeeds on day.
For all things and all worlds to quiescence
    Return, as the darkness of night;
And again reappear in their essence,
    As morning rekindles the light.
For the planets revolve in their courses
    And sing with harmonious chime,
The song of the conflict of forces,
    Of change, and the cycles of time.
And the seasons succeed in due order,
    And the sun seems to set and to rise,
As the earth spins along on the border
    Of that star-jewelled belt of the skies;
Where the stars in those far constellations
    Set forth, in twelve mystical signs,
The plan of the cosmic mutations,
    And the types of eternal designs.
While the forms, with eternities wreathéd,
    Come and go like cloud-shapes of an hour,
Fade to nought, and from nought are out-breathéd,
    As effects of some causative power,
That in whirlwinds of seeming confusion
    The vesture of being unfurled;
And wove, as a web of illusion,
    The visible world.

And as fixed as that law which constraineth
    In cycles all forms to appear,
A law through the ages remaineth
    To govern all things far and near.
'Tis that action produceth reaction,
    That no force can disappear;

THE
INELUCTABLE
CONSEQUENCES
OF ACTION

And the seed that is sown by the action,
    Bears fruit for a future year.
For the deed, once performed, never faileth
    To bring its results in its train.
The just act future blessings entaileth
    And the unjust involves future pain.
Thou, oh Zeus, who by strength overthrewest,
    In his kingdom, thy father of yore,
Dost thou think, if all things thou subduest,
    Naught can trouble thy reign evermore?
And ye Gods, whose vainglory would make you
    Sole lords of the height and the deep,
Do ye dream that no ills can o'ertake you?
    Do ye hope no requital to reap?
Ye have striven, with fury and passion,
    To conquer the thrones of the sky,
Ye have sought, in your madness, to fashion
    A might that could justice defy.
But the words of the prophecy spoken
    On the day when ye rose to your might,
Shall, as hands of that law never broken,
    Cast you down from this heavenly height.
Great ye seem in your power and glory;
    Ye are Gods, and your might is supreme;
But your splendour shall be but a story
    And fade like a dream.
    For ye, in strife for sovereign might,

THESE LAWS RULE Sought only conquest, caring naught for right;
EVEN THE GODS   And naught for heavenly lore.
So shall ye be o'erthrown in fruitless fight,
    As Titans were of yore.
And those two laws of cycles and of causes
    Shall for your deeds a just requital bring,

For the strong wave of cosmic change ne'er pauses,
 And every deed returns as in a ring.
For, as ye have Prometheus' counsel slighted,
And wronged him who brought conquest to your hands,
So, for your ill deeds ye shall be requited
 By law that ever stands.
And like the Gods of long ago,
 Whose might was built on shifting sands,
Ye shall be vanquishéd, and know
 Naught can avert what law demands.
And wisest of you all is he
 Who holdeth patience as a gem,
And weareth mutability
 Upon him as a diadem.

Zeus	Maidens, what mean the words that ye have sung?
Chorus	They mean what we have said, we come to warn
	Of what must come to pass. As ye have sown,
	So also shall ye reap. As ye o'erthrew
	The Titans and expelled them from their seats,
	So shall ye likewise lose your heavenly thrones.
Zeus	But how then know ye this must come to pass?
Chorus	Our eyes behold the future and the past
	Writ o'er the boundless pages of the skies.
	And yet, upon that awful scroll of fate,
	We can, alas, read but a few slight words,
	And these proclaim the doom of which we sang.
Zeus	But how, and when, and where shall it befall?
Chorus	Alas, we know not, we but comprehend
	Some flashes of the truth, we know not all.
	But one, methinks, approacheth to this height,
	Whose aspect speaks him bearer of a load
	Of grievous tidings. Thou, alas, mayest learn
	Too soon the knowledge that of us thou cravest.

(Enter Hermes)

Zeus	What tidings bearest thou from the realms of earth?
Hermes	Full heavy tidings, for that man whose fate
	I went there to discover, hath been slain
	By hands of evil men.
Zeus	I bid thee tell
	The manner and occasion of his death.
Hermes	The crime for which he died thou knowest full well.

'Twas blasphemy against the God of Heaven,
Since he, forsooth, was of them the sole one
Who did not so blaspheme. As for his death,
They brought him bound from out the dungeon cell
Where he had spent the night. A frantic throng
Went with him, cursing him for all the sins
Which they, not he, committed. On his brow
They placed a crown of thorns, and all the while
They mocked him, saying: "Hail, thou mighty king,
Thou soon wilt have thy kingdom." But he seemed
To heed it not and went with lofty mien,
As might a king, who, with triumphal pomp,
Returns victorious. As if, indeed,
His path led to a throne and not a cross.
Amid the throng one most of all I marked
Who cursed the guiltless prisoner; loud he hissed
Reviling names and spat upon his robe,
And said: "Die now, blasphemer, a just death.
Thou didst attempt to overthrow the rule
Of our most holy priests, and didst proclaim
That thou wert the redeemer of mankind.
Yea, thou didst further boast thou wert the son,
The son immortal of the most high God,
Only-begotten saviour. Let us see
If thou canst be immortal on the cross."
But he, in turn, replied: "Alas, my friend,

Why hatest thou me? I have no hate for thee.
No man I hate— All men I love and bless:
Even those who hate me, even thee I bless."
So passed he on. There is a little hill
Nigh to the city, bare of herb or tree,
And called "Place of a Skull" by natives there.
Here paused the throng, and here the soldiers fixed
The prisoner on a cross, and set it up.
With him they likewise crucified two thieves
And placed one on each side; above his head
They set a scroll naming him King. At this
The vulgar rabble who stood by laughed loud.
But lifting his sad eyes to heaven, he moaned:
"Forgive them, for they know not what they do."
And then the thief who at his left hand hung,
Mocked, saying: "If thou art the King, indeed,
Exert thy power, and save thyself and us."
Whereat the thief who at his right hand hung,
Rebuked the other: "We, at least, deserve
The doom we now receive, but he hath not
Done aught to merit it. He meets his fate,
A victim of the malice of the priests."
And then to him he said: "Oh mighty King,
Wilt thou think of me in the heaven-world?"
And he replied: "Thou wilt with me this day
Enter the heaven-world." At that the crowd
Grew silent. Then a weeping woman came,
And stood before the cross, and wailed aloud:
"Is it for this that visions seemed to show
My son as king of all the world? Alas,
In vain was all my mother-love for thee."
With that she fell upon her face and moaned,
But he said with calm voice: "Weep not for me,

Who shall this day win freedom from the cross
Of earthly life, but rather weep for those
Who still remain and suffer day by day,
Upon the cross of bodies crucified."
But now dark clouds spread o'er the face of heaven,
Hiding the orb of day, and a thick gloom
Fell on the earth, through which a sad voice rang:
"Oh God, my God, hast Thou deserted me?"
But called again soon after: "It is finished."
Here passeth a Great Soul, I thought, and turned
Unto the world to see if aught was changed
On his account, but in the neighbouring town
The people went about their daily tasks.
For here some mourners, solemn, sad, and slow,
Bore forth a corpse to its last resting place,
With dismal dirges. There, with dance and song,
A happy bridegroom led his happy bride
To their new home. Here tottered an old man;
And there a child wept o'er a broken toy;
Its mother struck it, and it wept the more.
In brief, the varied acts of human life
Are changed no whit, if great men live or die.

Zeus   Alas, alas, how blind are all mankind!
They mock their benefactors, and revile
The teachers who would lead their steps aright
Unto the light of truth. Such is the fate
Of every sage the world has ever known,
Since, for his deeds to help his fellow men,
He reaps as his reward curses and stones,
Hatred and loud revilings, and at length
A shameful death. Oh that it should be so!
But I can nowise find an help for it.

Hermes   Perchance 'tis that man doth but treat the ones

Who aid him, as thou didst thyself treat him
Who aided thee to win thy present throne?

Zeus   Remind me not of it. Full well I know
What evil then I did. How many times
Have I repented of it, yet I know
Repentence helpeth not a wrong once done.
But see, who draweth near:—why, can it be?
'Tis Hades! Long indeed hath been the time
Since he hath sought these halls. Some weighty cause
Indeed must urge him thus to leave the shades
And darkness that he loves, and come so far
Into the light he hates.

(Enter Hades)

My brother, hail!

What is it thou wouldst have me do for thee?

Hades   Zeus, hath the pledge, made firm 'twixt thee and me
What time we cast lots for the rule of earth,
Been broken? Can I rule the dead no more?
For flouted are the laws of my domain,
And my stern sceptre is a worthless wand
When none obey my bidding. Mighty Zeus,
Wilt thou deign to redress thy brother's wrong?
Or hast, forsooth, thy brother's rights forgot,
And deem'st the Gods no longer worthy rule?

Zeus   Why these unseemly taunts, my brother? Say
Wherein thy rights are broken or thy rule
Invaded, and who dares resist thy sway?
For, by Great Styx I swear, if any might
That the Supreme of Heaven can wield, avails
To win for thee redress for evils done,
Such might shall not be wanting to thine aid.
But first declare wherein thy rule is wronged.
What God or Spirit dares dispute thy power?

Hades No God it is, but a frail human ghost,
The shade of one who, being put to death
By the most shameful death of rebel slaves,
Comes now to me. Within the rayless realm
Of ghosts he walked, but from his brow there seemed
To shine a light which slew the ancient gloom.
No might or strength he used, but by soft words
He won all hearts unto him; not more power
Did Orpheus have when by his magic song
He charmed the doomed ghosts to forget their pain,
And me myself induced to pity him.
But this one sang not, nor called forth the voice
Of the most holy lyre, yet his words
Wrought strange effect: the furies, iron-souled,
Let fall their scourges, and the very flames
Stood still to hear him as these words he spake:
"I come to ransom from the bonds of sin
Whoso hath faith in me. The strength of hell
Before me cannot stand, nor death have power
On him who holds right faith. The Lord of Heaven,
Supreme, Omnipotent, All Just, All Pure,
Hath sent me to redeem the race of man
From this eternal prison, and the stains
Of primal sin are washed out with my blood."
Such words he spake as ne'er before were heard,
And all the shades flocked 'round him. Then I marked
What was most strange: he looked not like a shade
Of one who died, but rather like the ghosts
Of future things which yet shall come to be.
Then I addressed him: "Shade, dost thou not know
That I am ruler of this realm of shades?
Now, in the name of that most dreadful stream

Which bounds my kingdom, I command thee: tell
By what right or commission dost thou dare,
Without my sovereign sanction, thus to speak
Unto the subjects of my lawful power?"
He then replied: "I hold thy might as naught,
Thou Prince of Darkness; but that thou may'st know
Whose will I do, I tell thee, I obey
The Heavenly Father, in whose holy name
I hold thy power and all thy works, to scorn."
What thought I then? I thought that by his words
"The Heavenly Father" he could mean none else
But thee, who by all tribes of men art called
Father and King of Gods and all mankind.
And so I come to thee to ask what cause
Hast thou so to revoke mine ancient right?

Zeus My brother, I assure thee 'twas not I
Who gave this phantom power thus to raise
Confusion in thy realm, and thee defy.
'Tis true that while he lived I aided him
As much as fate allowed. He was, in sooth,
A wise and holy man, one who discerned
More of the truth than others of the age.
He ever worked for good, and he proclaimed
Unto bewildered and benighted men,
The Ancient Wisdom, which, through the dim past,
All holy sages taught. Yet what cause now
Impels this shade to slight thy rightful power
I cannot comprehend—

*(A rather long pause ensues, during which Zeus seems absorbed
in thought. Finally he is seen to start, and exclaims:)*

Ah, woe is me!
At last, at last, too clearly I behold

The long forshadowed doom. A light breaks forth
Within me, and the veil is rent away.
I see, I see, how man must pay the price
Of his past misdeeds, and how we ourselves
Must suffer for our errors— Far away
I see the spirit of Prometheus stand—
He speaks no word, but turns on me his eyes
That burn me with the thought of ancient wrongs.
How mad was I to think that the great wrong
I did to him could lightly be atoned!
I rede the riddle of his prophecy:
This shade have I begotten, even I!
And it shall be our doom; for by mankind,
The shade of that most just and holy man
Shall be mistaken for himself, and bring
Much sorrow on the earth; for men shall do
Great evil in his name, and in his name
The crafty bad and unenlightened good
Shall persecute the holy and the wise.
So shall this ghost be lifted far above
The Lords of Heaven, and we must wander far
Over the earth, dishonoured and unknown,
While a false god rules o'er the race of men,
Filling their hearts with divers miseries:
False terror and false hope, false grief, false joy,
Leading them far from out the path of truth.

Pallas   But canst thou not resist him? Is there naught
That we may do, lords as we are of heaven?
Must we, whose might cast down the Titan Powers,
Without one blow yield to an empty shade?

Zeus   Alas, in this our strength avails us not.
Strength cannot quell a phantom; there is naught
Whereby I see that we can conquer him.
          (Zeus is silent for a moment)

The veil is further drawn aside; I see
The cycle of his rule shall likewise end.
Then, with Prometheus' aid, I still have hope
We may regain our kingdom. But how long
'Twill be till this is done I cannot tell.
But meanwhile, let us not give way to gloom.
We still are Gods, whate'er may come to pass.
Yea, we are Gods, and we have yet to see
Whether, in sooth, this ghost of a false god
Shall, as he hopes, rule over all the earth.
Now let us fearless wait what comes to pass.

The Spirits Oh what is the secret of death?
of Cosmic   And where can one find,
Forces When man's body is left without breath,
                The light of his mind?
Oh what is the soul, the Self that still remaineth,
        And when the mortal frame
Returns to dust, its primal state regaineth?
        Is it for ay the same?
Or is man like the beasts of the fields that live to die,
        The plaything of chance and the sport of changeful things?
MAN, FROM Or doth he endure unchanged, like the Gods on high,
THE MATERIAL   Serene while eternities pass on pauseless wings?
STANDPOINT, For his mortal lives go past like the shadows of night
IS DOOMED   When the orb of day shines fair in the eastern sky,
But the works of his mind remain, like the changeless light
        That shines forever, though stars in their cycle must die.
And yet it seems a false hope lends him pinions,
        When he would rise secure
Above the Lords of Darkness whose dominions
        Throughout all time endure.

For with darkness in vain would contend
    What in darkness began,
And in darkness and nothing must end:
    The spirit of man.

The Muses   The secret of death is a change
    Which comes over all.
'Tis the veil 'twixt the known and the strange,
    But at length it shall fall.

THEY REVEAL   For birth and death are but a narrow portal
THE SECRET   Through which man's soul must go,
OF DEATH   His entrance and his exit as a mortal
    Unto the realms below.
For his birth in the world is a death in the realms of light,
    And his birth in the heavenly world is death on earth.
And so he is tossed about in ceaseless flight,
    Rolled on through his lives on the pauseless wheel of birth.
And yet he dares contend with the powers of gloom
    Because he knows that his spirit belongs to day.
And he fears not the strength of their hands or the might
        of their doom,
    But sets his feet unafraid on the perilous way.

AND PROCLAIM   And so 'tis no false hope bids him endeavour
THE ETERNITY   His freedom to attain,
OF SPIRIT AND   Because he knows his Self as that forever
ITS MASTERY   Conscious on every plane.
OVER DOOM   And with darkness by right would contend
    What in light first began;
And in light shall remain without end:
    The spirit of man.

The Spirits   Oh would that man might follow the righteous way,
    But yet his fate seems written across the skies
That far from the paths of truth his feet shall stray,
    Lured by a dark surmise.

For led by false beliefs for many a day
    He shall wander with sense confused in mental night,
Bewildered, lost, deluded, without one ray
    Of wisdom's light.

The Muses Though man may turn awhile from the way of truth
    He shall not wholly lose the sense of right,
Although the shadows of error and creeds uncouth
    May cloud his mental sight.
For in him the spark of an all-embracing ruth
    Shall cause that sacred light in his soul to shine
By which at length he shall know himself in sooth
    To be divine.

Both Shadows of a future day
    Flitting o'er the deeps of time,
What presage they? And what ray
    Shows us visions so sublime?
Faiths of darkness fade away,
    Words of light proclaim afar
Wisdom's re-established sway,
    Truth once more man's guiding star.
But the murky stream of years
THEY SURVEY   Sweeps like shade of night between,
A VISTA OF Dark with errors, dark with fears,
THE FUTURE   Dark with dreadful things unseen.
When will wisdom's light return?
    This to show our visions fail;
But we trust its spark may burn,
    And, at length, o'er night prevail.

*(Enter Phantasmus, followed by a host of shades
liberated from the Realm of Hades.)*

Zeus Ha! Thou pale phantom rising from the realms
Of endless night to seek our starry halls,

Thy looks proclaim defiance. Who art thou?
Speak, in the name of Him who Rules the Gods.

Phan.   I am the Christos who shall rule the earth.

Zeus   Chrestos thou may'st have been, but Christos, ne'er.

Phan.   Christos am I, anointed king of earth.

Zeus   I know what Christos is, that thou art not.

Phan.   Well, I am he whom men shall call the Christ.

Zeus   That canst thou be, but it concerns me not.

Phan.   Concerns thee not when I will seize thy throne?

Zeus   Phantom, reach not beyond a phantom's power.

Phan.   Thou art far more a phantom than am I.
Thy throne is reared on shadows, and thy might
Hath passed forever. In the name of Him
Whose hands first formed the world, He who protects
His chosen, and destroys their enemies,
He, Lord God of our Fathers, I command
Thee and thy fellow demons to forsake
This realm usurped by thine unlawful power.

Zeus   I am that Lord on whose name thou dost call
To drive me from my throne. What seekest thou?

Phan.   I seek my Father. Through the long, sad time
I dwelt on earth among the race of men
One hope bore up my heart. I thought at last,
When death had set me free from bonds of clay,
To meet my Heavenly Father face to face.
For, as I fasted in the wilderness,
When demon powers strove to lead astray
My heart with empty things, the thought of this
Made strong my spirit to resist their wiles.
And once, when preaching from a mountain height,
I seemed to see a ray of His Great Glory.
And for my Father's sake I dared defy
Crowned and enthroned iniquity, and bore

The crown of thorns, the scourges, and the cross,
Hoping at length to see the face of God.
Led by this hope I sought the rayless realms
Of awful night, where prisoned spirits mourned,
And strove to loose them from the bonds of death,
Proclaiming freedom in my Father's name.
But few, alas, would follow what I taught.

Zeus I am thy father. Whom else dost thou seek?

Phan. Oh God! I am derided! Can it be
This evil heathen tyrant is the pure
High God Jehovah, Israel's mighty King,
And father to my spirit, as I deem?

Zeus By many names am I on earth invoked
By many peoples, and the Hebrew race
Call me Jehovah. Unto Abraham
I gave the covenant, led his children safe
From their Egyptian bondage, and to Moses
Revealed a phase of universal truth,
And through succeeding prophets breathed my word.
So, by myself I swear, I am thy sire.

Phan. Begone, accurséd tempter! Thou art he
Who vexed my spirit in the wilderness.
Stain not with thy polluted lips the Name
Of the Most Holy. Thou art child of him
Whom my great Father cast in ruin down
The bottomless abyss, what time he raised
Rebellious war against Almighty Power.
My Father is the One, the Light of Light,
The God of God, Omnipotent and Pure.
Thou art a hellish serpent, soiled with sin,
Fit helper to the worm which dieth not.
Thou art set here to tempt me once again.
Begone, pollute the holy skies no more!

Zeus   Be not enraged, thou dost not comprehend
The things whereof thou speakest. Thou canst not
Do aught against me. Thou canst but pour forth
A flood of wrath, which may in future time
Recoil against thee. So, for thine own good,
I counsel thee, forbear unseemly words.

Phan.   Fiend, I defy thee, bidding thee once more
Get thee behind me, Satan. Stretch thine hand,
Pour forth the brimming vials of thy wrath
On this unshrinking head. A Child of Light
Sprung from the spirit of Almighty God
Need fear no rage of reptiles of the pit.

Zeus   Alas, what is it thou would'st have me do?

Phan.   Begone this instant from these heavenly halls!

Zeus   But what then wilt thou do when we have gone?

Phan.   I am the one who, as 'twas prophesied,
Will 'stablish an eternal realm of bliss,
The Christos-kingdom that shall last for ay.
Here, with these spirits who believe in me,
The souls I ransomed from eternal night,
I purpose in my Father's Name, to fix
A kingdom sempiternal, and to reign
Over the earth, until at length my Father
Shall stand revealed and from His judgement seat
Pass doom upon all beings.

Zeus   'Twill not be,
Thou art not Christos, thou art but a shade,
A phantom of the dead, and all thy realm
Shall be a realm of shadows. The true Christos
Is in each human soul, and his true kingdom
Is a pure mind. Thou wilt but by thine acts
Heap miseries upon the race of men,
And, in the end, thy rule shall be o'erthrown.

Now let us leave this place, the grain of doom
Is ripe for sickles of the fates to reap.
We can no more avert it. Let us go.

Phan. Aye, now ye do even as I desire.

*(The Gods slowly and solemnly rise from their seats and depart.
Pallas, as she goes, turns to Phantasmus and addresses him.)*

Pallas I am thy foe, and thou art foe to me.
We two will never hold divided sway.
Think not, that since we leave our former seats,
Our power hath passed away: there will be war
By thee against my followers, and in turn
By me against thyself. Thy spirit stands
Irreconcilably opposed to mine.
So thou canst know I will contend with thee
For rule over the mind and soul of man.

(Exit Pallas)

The Muses Beware, presumptuous being,
    Nor seize with reckless hand,
The might the Lord far-seeing
    Yields but at thy demand.
Recall how fate unbending
    Rewarded one of old,

THEY WARN
PHANTASMUS
AND CITE
THE EXAMPLE
OF PHAETON

And learn the dreadful ending
    Of actions overbold,
When Phaeton conceited
    To prove divine his sire,
And of the God entreated
    To drive his car of fire.
Behold, 'midst rays far-darting
    The youth resplendent stands.
He shakes the reins, and starting,
    The fiery steeds commands.

But than the youth far stronger
　　The fiery horses are;
They keep the road no longer
　　And headlong drag the car.

And now the fields of heaven
　　Are kindled by its rays,
And now, like falling levin,
　　It sets the earth ablaze.
Then Zeus, the Lord Unbounded,
　　Smote him to save the world,
And to the depths unsounded
　　Of sea his body hurled.
We know day's orb of glory
　　No fiery car can be.
And yet, in this old story
　　A mighty truth we see.
As from this tale the wages
　　Of rashness one may know,
That who in it engages
　　Doth sow the seeds of woe.
Then pause, oh Spirit daring,
　　And from rash deeds refrain,
Lest thou, through want of caring,
　　May'st find thy hopes in vain.

Who can foreshadow the years,
　　Or see in his mind as a glass
The burden of travail and tears
　　That man must suffer, alas!
The fury, the hatred, the fears
　　That the future shall bring to pass?

Not we, the daughters of song,
    Though the Lord of the might of the lyre
Hath taught us with vision strong
    To foresee what in time may transpire.
We can see but the shadows of wrong,
    And the lightnings of wrath as of fire.
For the years, like the waves of the sea,
    Roll on from the future and past.
As things which are not, they shall be,
    And the wrecks by that ocean upcast
It engulfeth, and nothing is free
    From change, and nothing stands fast.

(Exeunt the Muses)

PALLAS TRIUMPHANT

A LYRICAL DRAMA

DRAMATIS PERSONAE

Phantasmus . . . . *Who is called The Lord*

1st Messenger . . . . *An Angel*

Gabriel . . . . *An Archangel*

Michael . . . . *An Archangel*

2nd Messenger . . . . *An Angel*

Prometheus . . . . *A Titan, the Friend of Man*

Zeus . . . . *King of the Gods*

Pallas . . . . *Goddess of Wisdom*

Archangels, Angels and Spirits . . . .

The Gods . . . .

1st Chorus . . . . *The Angels*

2nd Chorus . . . . . . *The Spirits of Cosmic Forces*

3rd Chorus . . . . *The Muses*

Scene: Heaven.

The action commences in the morning.

Time: The End of a Cycle.

117

PALLAS TRIUMPHANT

*(The stage setting is the same as in the preceding drama.
Phantasmus is seated on the throne of Zeus. He is surrounded by
the Angels, some of whom, in the foreground,
constitute the Chorus.)*

The Angels   The passion and the flame of love
           Lift up our spirits to Thy throne.
     On rapture's wing we soar above
        The bounded regions of the known.
     Oh bliss ecstatic, in the light
          Of Thine high countenance to stand,
     Infinite justice joined with might,
          Mercy, with absolute command!
     Our eyes behold the suns of space:
          They are as darkness to Thine eyes!

THE ANGELIC   The lightnings of Thine holy place
CHOIR PRAISES
THE LORD   Outshine the light of endless skies.
     Before Thy light all lights are dark,
          Thy darkness past all light doth shine.
     E'en as a flame outshines a spark,
          Even so Thine effluence divine
     Shines through all worlds, for every star
          That gem-like gleams in deeps nocturnal,
     Proclaims Thy mercy near and far,
          The splendour of Thy glory's rays
     The majesty of might supernal,
          That fills the worlds with songs of praise.
     Naught is more blesséd than our Lord's
          Eternal glory to proclaim.

The highest bliss that heaven affords
 Is to adore Thine Holy Name.
Holy, holy, King of Light
 To Thee our songs we raise.
Oh glory in the highest height
 Thy Name alone we praise.

Creator, Saviour, Lord Eterne,
 Before the mystic birth of time,

THEY SING
OF CREATION

Alone Thy being's lamp could burn
 Within the uncreated clime.
And from the dark of utter naught
 Thy Word called forth the earth and sky,
And Angels into being brought
 To hymn Thine Holy Name on high.
Yet some of them against Thee rose,
 Whom Thou didst hurl to endless night,
And madest man, in place of those,
 To share with Thee the heavenly height.

THE FALL
OF MAN

But evil Satan from Thy path
 The erring feet of man beguiled
And on his head Thy righteous wrath
 Resistless fell and justice piled
Unnumbered sorrows on his soul:
 The fair-wrought earth Thine anger blasted,
And filled man's lifetime with much dole,
 Till for his sins he cried alone.
But though he sorely prayed and fasted,
 He could not anywise atone.

AND
REDEMPTION

But Thou, with mercy infinite,
 From bonds of hell didst set him free;
And by Thy blood's atoning might
 Redeemed whoe'er had faith in Thee.

Holy, holy, King of Light,
　　To Thee our songs we raise;
Oh glory in the highest height,
　　Thy Name alone we praise.
When Thou the angels didst create,
　　Formed by thy mighty Word divine,
We all adored Thine heavenly state,
　　Pleased to behold all glory Thine.

LUCIFER'S
REBELLION
AND HIS
PUNISHMENT But Lucifer, the child of dawn,
　　Dared Thine high lordship to despise,
And, by his pride to madness drawn,
　　Raised rash rebellion in the skies.
Then impious angels to his side
　　From all Thy realm made haste to fly,
And, lifted up by godless pride,
　　Thyself in battle dared defy.
But Thou, with might omnipotent,
　　Hurled the vile rebels from Thy throne,
To depths below the firmament,
　　In endless torment there to groan.
But when those wretches from Thy face
　　By Thy most holy wrath were hurled,
Thou sworest to fill their vacant place,
　　And so Thou didst create the world.
From naught in six brief days were made
　　The earth e'en as today it stands,
With all the heavens wide displayed,
　　They all were fashioned by Thine hands.
Thine holy will from nothing wrought
　　The heavens and earth still wrapped in sleep;
For earth was formless, void of aught,
　　And darkness brooded o'er the deep.

"Let there be Light!" Thy lips declare:—
 And there was light that slew the dark,
As o'er the mighty deeps laid bare
 Thy spirit shed a kindling spark.
These didst Thou part with mighty sway,
 And darkness sundered from the light.
And Thou didst call the light the day
 And called the darkness night.
Then Thou didst bid the waters all
 In one place brought together be,
And leave dry land, which Thou didst call
 Earth, and the waters called the sea.
On earth Thou then didst bid to grow
 Grass, trees, each green and growing thing;
Thy word was spoken, it was so.
 Lo! from the ground at once they spring.
Thine hands then formed the stars on high
 To mark the seasons with their ray,
And two great lights set in the sky
 As rulers of the night and day.
Thou madest fishes in the seas,
 And wingéd creatures of the air,
And beasts of divers kinds, all these
 Thou madest, that the earth doth bear.

THE WORK OF CREATION (margin note)

(Angels from one side)

Angels Oh Lord, a messenger doth seek
  Leave to approach Thine holy throne.
Phan. Let him draw near.
   (Enter Messenger)
    Thou mayest speak
  Thy will, and make thy mission known.

Mess.   Great Lord, give ear, there is a man on earth
Who doth deny creation in six days
Because, he says, 'tis written on the rocks
That many myriad rolling years passed by
Ere hills and valleys could be formed. Yet more,
He says that deep beneath the earth he found
The bones of primal monsters, such as now
Naught like exists on earth; and so he holds
That, since his calculations show long years
Had passed through which the strata of the rocks,
And silt and earth had covered them, and that
In other strata different forms appear,
It must be that long ages had elapsed
Between the first and later forms of life.
And more, he says that since succeeding forms
Differ but slightly from the forms before,
The one came from the other, and that Thou
Didst not, as we believe, form with Thine hands
All creatures, but that through the fixéd laws
Of nature they evolved, and ever comes
The complex from the simple, and the high
Succeeds the low. And so he says that God
Must be a spirit that must dwell within,
Informing and sustaining everything,
And not as Thou art, One who made the world
With Thine own hands, the visible agency
Of Triune Godhead. So he thinks, great Lord,
What doom is due to him?

Phan.   I bid my servants
Strive to convert him ere he meets his death.
For, if he dies without belief in me,
His portion is the Hinnom-Vale of fire,
Where never hope begins or torments end.
I am the gate unto eternal life.

Who trusts not me is worthy to be damned.
And yet I grieve that many souls of men
Must end in fire, since my words have not
As yet been spread to reach all ends of earth.
And e'en of those who hear my sacred words,
How many turn from them and choose the dark!
But let this word go forth to all mankind:
Who hath not faith in me is doomed to hell.

(Exit Messenger)

The Angels   Thou, in Thy wisdom's boundless plan,
                        Didst take the red clay of the earth,
THE CREATION   And in Thine image forméd man,
OF MAN   Lord of all creatures having birth.
                    Then Thou didst breathe into the clay
                        The breath of life, and man became
                    A living soul, to walk Thy way
                        And rule o'er Thy created frame.
                    For him a garden Thou didst make
                        With trees and every pleasant thing,
                    With fruits and streams his thirst to slake,
                        And blossoms of eternal spring.
                    O'er this fair realm dominion he
                        Might hold if he witheld his hands,
                    Nor plucked the fruit from off the tree
                        That in the midmost garden stands,
                    The tree whose branches bear on high
                        The fruit of knowing good and ill.
                    For man, Thou said'st, would surely die
                        If this he taste against Thy will.
HIS SUPREMACY   Man stood as king of earthly kind,
OVER THE   And to him all Thy creatures came:
BRUTE CREATION   He knew the lordship of his mind,
                        And gave to every beast a name.

AND HIS
LONELINESS
But when he saw Thy creatures all
    With mates to share their days,
On him the shadow seemed to fall
    Of his own lonely ways.
Then unto Thee he raised his voice
    And cried: "Lord God, how can it be
While all Thy beasts with mates rejoice,
    There is no fitting mate for me?"
Him in deep sleep Thou didst enfold

THE CREATION
OF WOMAN
    And took a rib from out his side,
Which Thou to woman's form didst mould,
    To be his helpmate and his bride.
Filled with Thine holy joy, the pair
    Together now their way did take.
They saw Thy glory everywhere,
    And sang glad praises for Thy sake.

THE MAN
AND WOMAN
ARE TEMPTED
BY SATAN,
COMMIT SIN,
AND ARE
ACCURSÉD
But Lucifer, now Satan named,
    A deadly stratagem devised,
And, as against Thy works he aimed,
    Himself in serpent's form disguised.
With promises of godlike power
    He tempted them with dark deceit,
And both, in an accurséd hour,
    Fatal forbidden fruit did eat.
When Thou didst view that deadly deed,
    Thy wrath made dark the light of day,
And lightnings of Thy might succeed
    The terrors of Thine awful sway.
An angel with a flaming sword
    Thou badest drive them from the tree,
Lest fruit of life should them afford
    The means to immortality.

Then sin and death like raging flame
    Against them rose, a deadly tide,
And wrath and sorrow on them came,
    The fruit of deeds unsanctified.
By labour of his hands, the man
    In sweat must eat his hard-won fare,
The woman, stricken by Thy ban,
    In sorrow must her children bear.
And that same curse of primal sin
    With all their seed abides for ay.
Oh who would ever dare begin
    To take that awful curse away?

(Angels from one side)

Oh Lord, Thy slave again doth seek
    Leave to approach Thine holy throne.
Phan.   Let him draw near.

(Enter Messenger)

          I bid thee speak
    And straightway make thy message known.
Mess.   There is a man among the sons of men
Who doubts the fall of man, and says that he
Evolved from lower things, and that his path
Is ever from the lower to the high.
And that it were unjust to punish man
For deeds due to his parents' ignorance
Five thousand years ago, since each must reap
The seeds sown by himself. And that, since so
There could have been no primal fall of man,
Redemption was not needed and that Thou
Wast but a mortal who taught men right acts,

And not the Very God of Very God.
And further, he declares that no such one
As Satan e'er existed; and that tales
Of rude rebellion rising in the skies,
Intestine war in Heaven, and rebels hurled
Into the pit of darkness, are no more
Than idle fables of the ignorant.
What shall be done to him?

Phan.   Let him likewise
Be cast into the Hinnom-Vale of fire
If he repent not ere his death. Oh men,
For you I died, to teach you holy truths.
Why do ye heed them not? For faith alone
In me can save mankind from endless flame.
I was ere the foundation of the world,
When stars of morning sang harmonious praise
And sons of God were joyful; I beheld
How Satan raised rebellion against God,
And how, defeated, he was headlong hurled
With ruin to the lampless wastes of hell.
And I was also present when first man
Was formed from the red earth, and know 'tis true
That he was made to take the place of those
With Satan hurled from Heaven, and I too saw,
Ah, woe is me! him tempted, and his fall.
Mine eyes beheld the sword of wrath unsheathed
To drive him from the paradise he lost.
And well I know the gloomy train of ills
That followed on his path, so whatso man
Thinks cannot help be false if it conflict
With words revealed by me, sole source of truth.

(Exit Messenger)

The Angels   Hail, Word of Light, which hath been ay,
               Is now, and ever shall be, Lord.
          To Thee the hosts of angels pray,
               In all the heights and depths adored.
          Though every leaf upon the trees
               Is as a tongue to sound Thy praise,
          And every drop in all the seas
               Doth strive Thine Holy Name to raise,
          Yet scarce the voices of the earth
               Can hint Thy glory in their songs,
          Nor rightly chanted is Thy Worth
               By endless hymns of angel throngs.
          What tongue is fit to name Thy Name,
               Ineffable in majesty,
          Transcending all the cosmic frame
               Which is but as a veil to Thee?
          Oh Thou of mercy passing thought,
               Justice, and holiness divine,
          All other mercy is as naught
               Beside the mercy that is Thine.
          Mourning the miseries of man
               Which justice could not take away,
          Thy mercy formed the awful plan
               Thyself their price of guilt to pay.
          Oh Thou most high, above all height,
               Beyond all depth adored,
          Whose glory is unchanging light,
               We praise Thy Name, oh Lord!
          Thou, the sole Lord of matchless sway,
               Before whose throne bow earth and sky,
          Didst take the humble garb of clay,
               Like human spirits born to die.

Thy Spirit did Thyself beget,
    And, of a Holy Virgin born,
Didst take upon Thyself the debt
    Of sin, that made the world forlorn.
E'en as a child Thy soul did yearn
    To find the holy and the true,
And Scripture meanings could discern
    More than the priestly order knew.
And older grown, Thou didst engage
    In fast, in penance, and in prayer,
Defiant to the Tempter's rage
    Whose wiles could not Thy soul ensnare.
Thou didst go forth among mankind
    To heal the sick and help the lame,

THE INCARNATION, Thou gavest sight unto the blind,
REDEMPTION,
AND VICARIOUS   And blessings unto all who came.
ATONEMENT And Thou didst teach the truth divine
    In words that ever shall endure,
A light forevermore to shine
    Upon the rock of doctrine sure.
The demons of the realms of night
    Fled trembling from Thy Word of Power,
The dead rose up before Thy sight,
    While lords of hell in darkness cower.
But oh! what tongue can e'er display
    The boundless mercy shown by Thee,
When Thou, to take man's sin away,
    Didst die his death of agony!
Like him didst sink to hell, but rose
    In three days victor o'er the grave,
Gaining eternal life for those
    With faith in Thy sole power to save.

That doom vicarious did win
    For man, through faith, the right to be
Redeemed from his ancestral sin—
    Unfathomable mystery.

(Angels from one side)

Great Lord, Thy servant seeks once more
    Some tidings unto Thee to bear.

Phan. Let him draw near, and as before,
    The message that he brings declare.

(Enter Messenger)

Mess. There is a man whose impious mind denies
Vicarious atonement, for he says
That no man can take on another's guilt
But each must answer for himself alone,
That since there never was a primal sin
There is naught to atone for, that if man
Were sinful, his sin must have come from Thee.
For, if Thou madest man, Thou must have made
Him perfect, else Thou 'rt not omnipotent.
And if omnipotent, and Thou didst make
Him subject unto sin, his guilt is Thine:
For, if a potter make a worthless pot,
The pot is not to blame, but he whose hand
Made it imperfect. And while some blame Satan
For spoiling Thy fair handiwork, this man
Asks: "Who made Satan? If Thou madest him,
How could ill pride have entered in his soul,
For who, pray, tempted Satan?" So this man
Derides Thy deeds and scoffs at holy things,
Saying that if man sins, Thy fault it is.
What is his fitting doom?

Phan.   Alas, alas,
How evil and ungrateful are mankind!
As for that man, I bid ye strive to show

To him the sin and folly of his ways.
For all mankind, inheriting the sin
Of their first parents, are condemned to meet
Eternal death and darkness, unless faith
In my atonement take away their guilt.
And then, alas, how many other sins
Since that first sin have men heaped on their souls!
Tempted by Satan they transgress yet more,
And all the Seven Deadly Sins embrace:
Pride, empty pride, that made the angels fall;
Covetousness, that sells its heart for gold;
Lust, foul with all the smirch of fell excess;
Anger, with frenzied eye and bloodstained hand;
Gluttony, swine-like, wallowing in the mire;
Envy, that turneth honey into gall;
And Sloth, in deadly torpor, kin to death.
But worse than these, that infidelity
Which questioneth the truth of Holy Writ,
Doubts if there be a God, or Heaven or Hell,
Or right or wrong, or anything at all
Unmoved and certain, but which tries all things
By reason's fading light, and finds them vain.
Thus men break down the pillars of the Law,
And undermine the temple of the Truth,
Taking away the basis on which stand
Virtue, religion, custom, government.
And so the people, left without a guide,
Woo perilous heresies, and all the world
Drifts on a sea of shifting circumstance
Towards blood and terror, anarchy and ruin,
While human souls, rejecting grace Divine,
Plunge headlong to the darksome depths of Hell,
Where dwell the fallen angels whom they serve.

For most men scorn my precepts to obey,
And wrong their fellow men with evil deeds;
While some, who seem right loyal to my faith,
Pervert it to an instrument of ill:
The people they mislead for their own ends,
And sell them poisonous doctrines for their gold;
While others, working outward righteousness,
Reject my teachings and against me turn,
Casting away their only hope of bliss.
For verily my Father, throned on high,
Hath it decreed that all the sons of men
Must sink into the fiery Hinnom Vale,
The outer darkness and the second death,
Except they win salvation through their faith.
Alas, the world is no more as of old,
When my Great Church outstretched her healing hands
Over the nations, when e'en kings obeyed
The Word of God, when knights of God went forth
To right all wrongs, to seek the Holy Grail,
Or bear unto benighted heathen lands
The lamp of faith, the sword of righteousness.
For now all faith is fallen to decay
And my True Church is well-nigh desolate:
No more do rulers heed religion's voice,
Nor any sword is lifted to defend
The Faith against the hordes of Heathenesse.
Alas! I know not what to do to save
Mankind from plunging headlong to its doom.
For I myself can nowise find the power
To stem the tide of boundless sinfulness.
It was revealed to me that if I died,
Sinless, to take away the whole world's sins,

That such vicarious sacrifice might atone
For those with faith in it: yet here it fails,
The faith is wanting, for where'er we turn
Men go still further from the saving faith.

Mess. Oh mighty Lord, what should Thy servant do?
Phan. "What should I do?" Thou askest, what to do?
Alas, I know not, for men have no faith
In the Most Holy Doctrines, through which lack
In nowise can they 'scape the endless fires.
No more do men curb heresy with zeal,
Wanting themselves the faith from which zeal springs;
And heresy brings men to hopeless doom.
Yet I myself have failed to re-illume
Religion's lamp, how sore howe'er I strove.
Oh, would that my great Father, hid too long,
For whom in vain these weary eyes have yearned
These long two thousand years, whose strength alone
Can set aright the tangled deeds of men,
Oh would that in the end He might reveal
Himself unto the world, and stand as judge
Between the quick and dead on that dread day
When, blasted by the final trump of doom,
The heavens and earth shall pass like smoke away,
And souls stripped naked strive in vain to hide
Their crimes from the relentless eye of Truth,
While all creation, brought before His throne,
Falls trembling at the awful might of God.

(Exit Messenger)

The Angels Alas, that faith decays,
　　　Alas, that zeal grows cold.
Earth rings no longer with Thy praise
　　　As in the days of old.

The days when words of thine
    Were reverenced everywhere,
And from each cloister, cell, and shrine,
    Arose the voice of prayer,
When men held worship dear,
    And wrought in piety,
As generations toiled to rear
    Majestic shrines to Thee.
There, where dim light is cast
    Through stainéd windows fair,
Beneath the Gothic arches vast,
    Through incense-laden air,
With pomp of solemn rites,
    Incense, and lights, and song,
With crucifer and acolytes,
    Slow moves the priestly throng,
While to deep organ-tones
    The choral chants reply,
The priest the blesséd Mass intones,
    And lifts the Host on high.

But ah, the world declines
    Through gloomy latter days,
And men, neglecting warning signs,
    Persist in sinful ways.
No saints now offer prayer
    In desert, cave, or cell,
No longer men to church repair
    When peals the holy bell.
No longer as of old,
    The knights embattled ride,
Their armour gleaming bright with gold,
    To quell the paynims' pride.

THEY TURN
WITH NOSTALGIA
TO THE FAITH
OF THE PAST

THEY DEPLORE
THE DECLINE
OF FAITH

No more do men of God
        Thine holy laws fulfill,
And smite with torture's sternest rod
        The ones who scorn Thy will,
Or filled with zeal Divine
        To vindicate Thy name,
The witch and heretic consign
        Unto avenging flame.
For all mankind hath turned
        From Thy sublime decrees,
And faith and piety are spurned
        For worldly vanities.

THEY IMPLORE
DIVINE
RETRIBUTION
ON THE
INFIDELITY
OF THE WORLD

Oh Lord in Thy splendour enthronéd,
        Look forth upon earth and behold
The great sins of mankind unatonéd,
        And the evils of errors untold.
For men turn from the light of Thy teaching
        To the darkness of doubt and dismay;
Neither stretch they the hands of beseeching,
        Nor bend they to pray.
And Thy Church, which of yore stood exalted,
        With the healing of men in her hands,
Is cast down, and her mercies are halted
        By the power of infidel bands,
Since man turns to old faiths and acc urséd
        Strange doctrines by Satan proclaimed,
Dark creeds long ago wide-disperséd,
        Ere Thy Name had been named,
While some rise in the vain aspiration
        To be saved through good works of their own,
And forget man is granted salvation
        At the price of Thy mercy alone.

But we bow to Thy Name, and obey Thee,
    Great Lord, God of God, King of Kings,
And in fear and humility pray Thee,
    By all holy things:
By Thy splendour which shines through the ages
    Reflected by martyr and saint,
Men who dared any task for faith's wages
    And whose zeal neither cooled nor waxed faint,
By the Cross with Thine agony shaken,
    By Thy blood, by the tears of Thine eyes,
By that hour when by mercy forsaken,
    Earth grew dark at Thy cries.
We beseech Thee, to those who adore Thee,
    Come thou in Thine infinite might,
And who bows not in reverence before Thee,
    Let him perish in ultimate night
On the day when Thy terrors unbounded
    Are loosed, and all things pass away,
When the trumpets of Judgement are sounded
    Before the New Day.

(Enter Messenger)

Mess.   Oh mighty Lord, o'er all the realms of earth
Mankind turns from Thy ways, faith is no more
Either in Thee, Thy Mercy, or Thy Justice,
Or any heavenly power of righteousness.
And, if men still have faith in anything,
'Tis in those evil doctrines which before
I told Thee of. For all their hearts and souls
Are set on wealth and power. Some of them
Heap up vast treasures of pernicious gold
Wrung from their fellow men, while others strive
With brutal force to overthrow the right.

Even the mighty nations of the world
Still seek by force each other's overthrow.
For, first despising Christian brotherhood,
They vied in forging arms of earthly power,
Trusting in transient things, and from the poor
Wrung the last mite in soul-destroying toil
To fashion deadly engines, and meanwhile
Fanned flames of mutual hatred. In their midst
There was a nation, mighty, young, and bold,
Valiant in warlike might and deeds of arms,
Yet seeking the more lasting gains of peace.
But evil counsels turned it from Thy ways.
Then many men met fighting, and the ground
Grew red with blood, while fiery darts were hurled
Which laid waste Thine high temples. Hate and rage
Spread like a raging torrent o'er the earth,
So that most diverse portions of mankind
Joined in the mingled fray. For years they fought
On land, on the wide spaces of the sea,
Yea, e'en beneath the waves and in the skies,
Wasting vast wealth in devastating strife.
And many died, though pestilence and famine
Reaped larger harvests than the hand of man.
The toil of years, the gains of centuries,
The garnered treasures of the olden times,
Were swept away, or scattered to the winds,
And mighty nations fell in that dread fray.
At length the conflict ended in what seemed
The triumph of the right, but those who won
Sought vengeance on the vanquished; with harsh terms
They crushed the helpless people of their foes.
Then the rebellious spirits of mankind
Rose in their wrath. The lowly and the poor

Seized power from the mighty, and o'erthrew
The ancient order, anarchy and ruin,
Rage, hatred and despair, destructive strife,
Are everywhere; religion is no more.
Men scoff at God, blaspheme against Thy Name,
And hestitate no more at any sin.
So fares the world. Oh Lord, what should we do?

Phan.   Oh utter depth of hopeless misery!
Lord God Jehovah, Heavenly Father, hear!
For twice a thousand years with endless prayer
I have invoked Thy mercy. Thou didst make
Me to be Thy Messiah, and I bore
Unmurmuringly ignominy and death,
And won this throne for Thee from the fell fiend,
And strove to win mankind to praise Thy name.
But Thine own face mine eyes have never seen.
My prayers and intercessions win Thee not
To aid me. Art Thou then so wroth with me?
For but a few men praise me in Thy Name,
And they are oftentimes the worst of men,
Who rob, burn, slay, and do whatever things
I taught them while on earth they should not do.
And 'mongst mankind the noblest and the best
And wisest doubt Thy power and deny
My mission to redeem the sins of man.
So, therefore, gloomy hell must be their home,
For no man may attain the crowns of heaven
Save through his faith in me. And cruel wars
They wage, and waste the substance of my Church,
And drown fair mercy's voice in cries of hate.

(Voice, offstage, of the Leader of Second Chorus,
The Spirits of Cosmic Forces)

Leader   Then doth thy soul recall the words of Zeus?
Phan.   Satan, begone! Wouldst tempt me yet again?
Leader   Whom callest thou Satan? No such one we know.
Phan.   Satan is whatsoever tempteth me,
          And such thou art—

(Enter the Spirits of Cosmic Forces)

                       But what beings are ye,
      And by what right seek ye the throne of heaven?

Chorus II   We are the spirits of changeless power,
          Of Cronus we saw the doom forlorn.
      We warned Great Zeus of thy destined hour,
          And we warn thee now that thy times are gone.
Phan.   Swift get ye gone from this heavenly hall,
          For ye are heathen spirits, I ween,
      And know ye I am the lord of all
          Save one, whom mine eyes have never seen.
Chorus   Far, far in the darkness whence all things came,
          We watched the birth of the things which are,
      When the dust that fashioned thine earthly frame
          Was whirling flame of a flaming star.
Phan.   Ye lie, for my spirit endured for ay—
          And your words and your vaunts are naught to me—
      As I stood with the spirit of God that day
          When the world arose from the primal sea.
Chorus   The world that thy god of nothing wrought
          Is but in the fancy of thy mind
      Which seeth alone the things that are naught,
          And unto the things that are is blind.
Phan.   But who be ye? I recall not now
          If aught like you I did ever see.
      Yet if sooth be the words ye speak, Oh how,
          I bid you say, may they come to be?

THE PERSONIFIED
LAWS OF NATURE
DEMAND
RECOGNITION

THEY CONFRONT
THE FANTASTIC
FABLES OF
SUPERSTITION
WITH THE
FACTS OF
COSMIC PROCESS

Chorus   Dost thou not recall that dreadful day
When thy soul went forth from the form of clay,
When, defying the might of the Lords of Doom,
Thou didst rise on high from the realms of gloom
And madest thy way
To heights where the light of glory lay?

Dost thou not remember the forms of might
Clothed in the splendour of living light,
Whose tongues spake forth the warning word,
The omens of doom that thine ears have heard,
Foretelling thy night?
Have all these things been forgotten quite?

THEY REMIND
PHANTASMUS
OF THE PAST

Holds thy mind no thought of that God on high
In thy father's name whom thou didst defy,
And didst spurn and taunt him with words of hate?
But who warned thee still of thy coming fate,
Which is now drawn nigh,
When thy throne shall shake with the shaken sky?

Dost remember the tale of that youth o'erbold
Who the reins of the Sun-God's car would hold,
How he swerved aside and was headlong hurled
'Midst the ruin and flame of a flaming world?
How to thee was told
That thy doom might follow the dooms of old?

THEY DECRY
THE EVILS OF
SUPERSTITION

But in spite of the warnings thou didst proclaim
Thyself as lord of the world's vast frame.
Thou drovest the Gods from before thy face
And didst set up phantoms in their place
Who should praise thy name,
That the skies might ring with the noise of the same.

So, for years that passed on the wings of night
Thou didst sit enthroned on the heavenly height
While the darkened realms of the earth were rife
With phantoms of terror and anger and strife,
Waxing great in thy sight
As the clouds that cover the day's fair light.

Thy servants went forth to divers lands
And bore thy faith unto strange, far strands;
While the heathen tribes that have turned to thee
Win a guerdon of trouble and misery.
For the gifts of thine hands
Are shadowy terrors and stern commands.

Man's soul thou wouldst fetter with steel and fire,
Thou wouldst quench in the dust his heart's desire,
As a worm of the dust thou wouldst have him be,
Crushed to earth with the thought of humility;
Nor to aught aspire
Save to praise thy name with the heavenly choir.

AND PREDICT
THE DOWNFALL
OF THE KINGDOM
OF UNREASON

But Time, in his endless winnowings,
Drives the years like chaff with the wind of his wings,
And the ripened grain of doom doth smite
From the chaff of the ages in swirling flight—
The harvest that springs
In the desolation of transient things.
And the harvest of doom that Time reaps shall be
The doom of the end of thy tyranny—
For at length from the ages is come that day
When the strength of thy kingdom shall pass away

And mankind be free.
For the measure of fate is fulfilled for thee.

(Enter Messenger)

Mess. Oh master! hear the evils of mankind—
The final day is come, behold their hosts
Drawn up for combat, all the kings of earth
Have called their hosts to battle, all mankind
Stands ranged beneath their banners, and 'tis not
For Thee they fight, to make Thy will prevail,
But rather to oppose Thine holy will
And overturn the kingdom of Thy Name.
For Antichrist hath risen in their midst,
And those false gods whom Thou didst drive afar,
Have come once more to power, and mankind
Is shouting: "Let the darkness pass away.
Hail to the light of Wisdom, hid too long
But once again revealed! No more we bow
In homage unto images of stone,
Or images of dogma and of creed.
We worship not the idols but the Light,
That Light supernal, which beyond all creeds,
Beyond all rites and legends ever shines,
And guides mankind upon the path to Truth."
This I construe to mean that they despise
Thine holy will, and therefore it is meet
Thy flaming sword should not too long repose
Within its peaceful scabbard. Lift Thine arm,
Oh mighty Lord, and smite Thine enemies.
Phan. From that which thou hast said, I do not deem
The final day hath dawned, nor do I hold
That Antichrist himself hath risen up

To lead the armies of our enemies.
It rather seems these men have been misled
By the false teachings of those wicked men
Who doubt my teachings; and, if this be so,
They are unworthy for mine arm to smite.
Yet, lest this new rebellion wax too great
Through weighing lightly its increasing strength,
Methinks 'twere well to call right suddenly
A solemn synod of th' angelic powers.
Let them be straightway summoned to my throne.

The Angels Ye leaders of the angel-bands,
     Ye princes of the realms of light,
   Hark, what the Blesséd Lord commands
THEY BROADCAST   And hitherwards direct your flight.
A SUMMONS The message which our lips intone
TO COUNCIL   Shall pass beyond the day and night,
   And summon you before the throne.

(Enter Gabriel, Michael, and other Archangels)

Gabriel Oh Master of Mercy! Thy summons afar
     Brings Thy servant swift-passing the luminous way.
Michael As the splendour that streams from a bright-flaming star
     Is the light of Thy Will, that Thy servants obey.
Phan. Oh faithful servants, bulwarks of my kingdom,
   Because I am perplexed I summon you
   For counsel in the stress of evil times.
   Behold, through all these years the race of man
   Rebels against my teachings and defies
   My righteous will. Long have men lived in sin,
   Deriding all commandments of the law
   In secret, though with specious reverence
   Protesting their lip-service; but of late

E'en this is wanting, and their lips declare
That which was in their hearts; but still more ill
The tidings which my servant brings this day.
For now, he says, men turn to open war
Against me, and with might of impious arms,
Oppose the very sovereignty of God.
Now therefore since in spite of mine endeavours,
The world doth nowise yield unto my will,
I crave your counsel what 'twere best to do,
To make the Kingdom mighty in the world.

Gabriel Oh Holy Saviour, even in the dust
My spirit bows in worship at Thy Name.
How, then, can the most wretched race of men
Dare to oppose Thy statutes? It doth seem,
Oh gracious Lord, to Thine unworthy slave,
That man no longer merits any grace.
Therefore let trumpets of the Doom be blown,
Let heaven and earth be shaken, let Thine hosts
Go forth to the last battle, then, perchance
Thy long-foreshadowed triumph may arrive.

Michael Sweet Fountainhead of Mercy, deign to lend
A gracious ear to my most humble prayer:
Suffer Thy servant, even I, to lead
A portion of the heavenly host against them.
So, if they be but mean and worthless foes,
Our hands shall quickly work their overthrow.
But if, indeed, this be the godless host
Of Antichrist, and this the final field
Of Armageddon, let the trump of doom
Be sounded, and Thou could'st Thyself lead forth
The rest of the embattled host of heaven
Against these infidels, and smite them down,
And pass Thy judgement upon all the world.

Phan.   I weigh thy counsel well, and think it good.
        Go, Michael! Lead the battled hosts of heaven,
        But show our foes thy mercy. First command
        That they cast down their weapons and repent
        In sackcloth and in ashes; let them bow
        Unto the very dust, and humbly pray
        For mercy, vowing with most weighty vows
        To do my will and to accept my faith
        Thenceforward and forever; but if they
        In insolence of pride refuse to yield,
        Unsheath thy sword, and slay them every one,
        And cast their souls into the Hinnom Vale,
        The outer darkness, and the sea of fire
        Which is the second death, where hope is not,
        Where the worm dies not, nor the flame is quenched.
        This being done, return to bear me word.

Michael   Oh mighty Lord, I joy to do Thy Will.

            (Exit Michael)

Gabriel   Great Lord, what is it Thou wouldst have me do?
        Shall I sound forth that trumpet o'er the world
        That calls the sheeted dead out of their graves?
        Or shake the heavens with resistless might
        'Til stars are strewn on earth, and the bright sun
        Wax dim and lusterless? Or shall I loose
        The winds from the four corners of the world
        In furious tempests, bid the seas arise
        From their appointed bounds and cause the earth
        To quake and tremble as if palsy-stricken?
        Or shall I rather cast down flames from heaven
        And loose the fire that slumbers at earth's heart
        'Til all this universe be quite consumed
        In the dread flames of Thine avenging wrath?

Phan.   Nay, 'tis not time to let these woes descend
          Upon mankind, the times are not fulfilled.
          I rather bid thee go and call together
          The angels who shall make up Michael's host.
          See that they be prepared for deadly strife.
          This done, return, and wait my next command.
Gabriel Oh Lord, to do Thy will is our delight.

                    (Exit Gabriel)

The Angels   Behold, the day of wrath is here,
                    The day the Sovereign Lord
THE   Against the wicked shall appear
HEAVENLY HOST   With His avenging sword.
ASSEMBLES   In mail that gleams as lightning's glow
                    Or like the orb of day,
               The angel hosts to battle go
                    In terrible array.

          *(Voices sounding faintly, as from a distance, sing
               The Battle Hymn of The Angelic Army)*

          Holy, Holy, Holy,
               Our Lord whose arm is sure
          To smite to depths most lowly
               The hosts of hearts impure.
          The arméd hosts of heaven
               Are marching to the fight,
          With swords like flames of levin,
               With armour gleaming bright.

               (Angels in the foreground)

          Thy leader Michael goes before,
               His sword is as a flame;
          The tribes that would not Thee adore
               Shall tremble at the same.

Yea, all the wicked host shall shake
    Before that mighty sword,
Yet far more terribly they quake
    At Thy dread wrath, Oh Lord.

(From a distance, but louder than before)

Holy, Holy, Holy,
    Thrice blesséd be Thy Name,
Thy servants chanting lowly
    Still glorify the same.
Yet creatures of an hour,
    Whose life is as a breath,
Rebel against Thy power,
    Oh Lord of Life and Death!

(Voices grow louder)

But we, who bow before Thee
    And praise Thy matchless worth,
Will make mankind adore Thee
    Or hurl it from the earth!
Like to the lamps nocturnal
    That gem the galaxy,
Or days of the Eternal,
    Or waters of the sea,
Or leaves on trees that slumber,
    Or sands of the sea-coast,
So far beyond all number,
    The numbers of our host.
And as the blazing levin
    A mighty tree would fell,
So shall our hosts of heaven
    Destroy the brood of hell!

(Voices become fainter)

Holy, Holy, Holy,
   We praise Thee morn and night,
With hearts most meek and lowly
   Thy foemen shall we smite.

(Enter Gabriel)

Gabriel   Most gracious Lord, a mighty host is armed
In adamantine mail; some of them bear
Keen two-edged swords, as bright as lightning flame,
That gleam right terribly, and others wield
Spears of bright gold with heads of diamonds;
While all of them have broad and lustrous shields
Like to the noonday sun, and as they flew
With rainbow-tinted wings spread to the light,
It seemed as if the radiant stars of heaven
Shot from their spheres, or else as if there flowed
A broad, swift river of light across the skies,
The foam of which was flame, and gleaming stars.
So great the splendour of the heavenly host.

Phan.   'Tis well, now they go forth to fight our foes—
And thee I bid go with them, but forbid
That thou should'st mingle in the fight. So soon
As thou canst tell who is victorious,
Return with thy most instant speed to me
To bear me tidings of the chance of war.

Gabriel   Dear Lord, right hard is the command Thou layest
Upon me, for, as I behold the light
And glory of the conflict, I too yearn
To lay the good sword on our enemies.
Natheless, as Thou hast bidden shall I do.

(Exit Gabriel)

The Angels   Now, at last, from the ages unnumbered,
        Is come that retributive day
When Thy sword, which in mercy long slumbered,
        Makes ready to slay
All the hosts of the sinners, defying
        Too long the dread flame of Thine ire,
Which is kindled for vengeance undying,
        As a ravening fire.

THE ANGELS   Ah God, Thou whose mercy unbounded
ANTICIPATE   Shines forth on the blest evermore,
ARMAGEDDON With what terrors shall those be confounded
        Who scorn to adore!
Now they stand in the pride of defiance,
        And vaunt in the lust of their might:
"By the light of our infidel Science
        The world shall be bright."
But their wisdom to folly Thou turnest,
        Their pride to destruction shall fall,
With the flame of Thine anger Thou burnest
        Their works, one and all.

THE DAY   They shall seek, when that doom comes upon them,
OF WRATH   In vain from those torments to flee.
They shall pray for the crags to fall on them,
        To hide them from Thee.
They shall humble themselves in their terror
        Who late were so proud in their sin,
They shall claim, in their madness of error,
        The beasts as their kin.
They shall gaze at the skies thunder-riven,
        And call on Thy mercy, oh Lord.
But for them shall no sins be forgiven;
        Thy wrath is a sword

That shall harry them all through the portal
    Of stark, unendurable hell,
In the regions of anguish immortal
    Forever to dwell.
For Thy Judgement on them hath descended,
    The dread day of doom is at hand,
When the works of all times shall be ended,
    And nothing shall stand.

AND THE LAST
JUDGEMENT

Can we sing of the infinite sorrows
    That come with that terrible day?
The anguish no pitiful morrows
    Shall e'er take away?
For their hopes shall be blasted forever,
    And all upon earth shall be sad,
As Thy Justice remorseless shall sever
    The good from the bad.
From the mother the child shall be taken,
    The husband and wife rent apart,
And the lover left lorn and forsaken
    In anguish of heart.
For the partings shall then be eternal,
    And never a hope come to those
Condemned to the regions infernal,
    Prepared for Thy foes.
But a few, signed and sealed to salvation,
    Thine elect, chosen ages ago,
Shall escape the eternal damnation
    And infinite woe.
They shall rise to the regions of gladness,
    Their toils and their conflicts are o'er,
And the shadow of pain or of sadness
    Shall touch them no more.

Where forever the songs of the blesséd
    Ring 'round the White Throne where Thou art,
And a rapture by words unexpresséd
    O'erflows from each heart
Of the host in the regions eternal,
    The sinless and glorified band,
Who, adoring Thy splendour supernal,
    Forever shall stand.

The time that long had seemed so far away,
    At last hath come to be.
The hosts of God and Satan meet today—
    The wicked can but flee.
And then, at last, when fought is that dread fray
    Of Armageddon, Thou wilt rise in might
To hold forevermore unquestioned sway,
    And end earth's final fight.
For o'er Thy vanquished foemen Thou wilt stand
    To pass on them the dooms of sovereign right,
And hurl them, at the stretching of Thine hand,
    Unto eternal night.

The Spirits Oh ye spirits whose hopes are exalted
    By the strife that ye deem ye have won,
Do ye trust at your words shall be halted
    The earth in her dance 'round the sun?
THE POWERS Do ye hope at the noise of your crying,
OF NATURE
CHALLENGE   The tides of the fathomless sea
THE EFFICACY May be stayed, or the clouds heaven-flying
OF MIRACLES
TO SUBVERT   No longer be free?
THE ORDER OF Do ye think that the stream seaward flowing
NECESSITY
    Shall be turned and flow back to its source,
Or that winds of the sky ever blowing
    Shall stop in their course?

Or perchance that the stars without number,
 The sands of Eternity's shore,
At your bidding shall fall into slumber
 And thence be no more?
Yea, forsooth, by mere words ye shall master
 The heavens, the earth, and the sea,
And the universe fill with disaster,
 Ere this thing may be:
That mankind, having bid you defiance,
 Should bow once again to your might,
And the lamp of their dearly-won Science
 Be quenched in your night.

Now the world doth your bidding no longer,
 All things hold their ways firm and fast;
Yet ye trust that your words shall be stronger
 To call back an age that is past.
For ye seek to turn back the remorseless
 Swift wings of the years as they fly,
But your words against time remain forceless,
 As ages go by,
As, with steeds spreading rainbow-hued pinions,
 In cars like the lightnings that burn,
The Hours speed through your dominions,
 And never return.
For the day of your rule hath departed,
 When all held in awe your decree;
And those once but your slaves, and faint-hearted,
 Stand fearless and free,
With no dread of the conflict impending,
 Nor fearing your powers at all,
They resolve to abide to its ending,
 And triumph or fall.

Though ye trust that your might never faileth,
    And deem that the outcome is known,
Yet beware, lest the host that prevaileth
    May not be your own.

THE COSMIC
POWERS PREPARE
FOR CONFLICT

For behold, the earth is hidden
    As far o'er the fields of the sky,
On winds by the storm-clouds ridden,
    The tempest draws nigh.
As an army breathing slaughter
    Goes forth to the battle plain,
The children of air and of water,
    The kindred of mists and of rain,
Spread over the regions of heaven,
    And cover the face of the light;
Then forth leap the flames of the levin
    With terrible might.

(During the singing of the preceding verses, storm clouds appear,
the scene grows dark, lightning and thunder follow)

THE SPIRITS
TAUNT
PHANTASMUS
ON HIS
IMPOTENCE
AGAINST THE
POWER OF
THE LIGHTNING

And the lightning makes thee tremble
    Like a slave before whips of steel!
Though the hosts of the skies assemble
    At the foot of thy throne to kneel,
And praise thee with songs unending
    As the lord ever reigning on high,
While the angels in arms stand defending
    The holiest throne of the sky,
Yet fear comes upon thee, beholding
    That radiant birth of the gloom,
And its flashes afar seem unfolding
    Some glimpse of an immanent doom.

For thine hands never wielded the levin,
     Though thou as a god wert hailed;
While thou sittest aloft in heaven,
     O'er thy temples it still prevailed.
And though prayers like the leaves were scattered
     And baptism given their bell,
Thy loftiest spires were shattered
     By the flames that upon them fell.
And the priest that bowed to adore thee
     The lightning perchance would slay,
For the might that it flashed before thee
     Thy bidding would not obey.
So 'twas fabled a foe defied thee:
     "The Prince of the Power of the Air"
Whose impious spirit denied thee
     And recked not of curse nor of prayer.
And in vain didst thou place reliance
     On these 'gainst the thunder's crash,
For no hands save the hands of Science
     Can check the impending flash.
And the law that thy lips proclaiméd
     Was not the law that could bind
The powers by thee untaméd
     That bow to the will of mankind.
For man in these days no longer
     Shall worship a shadow's name;
The might of his mind is stronger
     Than all that would sway the same;
And above the stroke of the lightning,
     The fury and strength of the gales,
As a light in the gloom slow-brightening,
     His wisdom prevails.

For the forces that make thee cower,
 His soul shall in no wise fright:
The lightning shall yield its power
 Unto the hands of his might.
It shall speed him swift on his faring,
 It shall turn the night into day;
It shall labour, his burdens bearing,
 And smooth the path of his way.
It shall sing his babes to slumber,
 It shall spread his words through the land,
It shall serve him in ways without number,
 And answer his least command.
He rears up his lofty towers,
 Yet not to make great thy name,
But to wield the might and the powers,
 The voice of the lightning flame!
The voice that on wings of thunders,
 Far, far o'er the widespread lands
And shores that the ocean sunders,
 Flings far his high commands;
Though between them the dim sea darkens,
 And tempests rage in the sky,
As one sitteth alone and hearkens
 For the sound of a far-flung cry.
And it comes—through the gloom storm-shaken
 The words of man take flight,
And the answering deeps awaken
 Across the void of the night.
He shall fashion him engines dire
 Of strange and gigantic form,
With sinews of steel and fire
 And strength like the strength of the storm.

The might of the rushing river,
    The force of the winds and the tides,
The lightnings that flash and quiver,
    With fire and steam besides,
Shall serve him with toil unceasing
    And ever his thoughts obey,
The strength of his hands increasing
    And spreading the bounds of his sway,
While his creatures of copper and iron,
    The mighty machines of his hands,
Shall with limitless power environ
    The place where he stands.

THEY
INTERPRET IT
AS AN
OMEN OF
FUTURE EVENTS

And as lightning, whose dreadful power
    Puts fear in the soul of thee,
Shall yield, in a coming hour,
    His servant to be,
So the forces that now spread terror
    Shall bow to the strength of his will.
He shall conquer the stronghold of error
    And vanquish the powers of ill.
For man like a God shall master
    All things that were hidden in night;
The world of his knowledge grows vaster
    And vaster his might,
While the light of his wisdom transcendent
    Illumines all mysteries blind,
And makes all the cosmos resplendent
    With radiance born of the mind.

(Enter Gabriel)

Gabriel Great Lord, preserve us! We beseech Thine aid!
Phan.   What! Have not all our foes yet been destroyed?

Gabriel	Alas, no! They have thus far been triumphant!
Phan.	Ye hosts, prepare for battle, arm yourselves—
	And let mine armour, wrought for this last fray,
	Be brought from heaven's eternal armoury!
	Ye angels of the trumpets, stand prepared
	To sound the blasts of doom, and let the Powers
	Of Fire, and Flood, and Earthquake, and Great Storm,
	Prepare to loose their woes upon mankind.
	Set all in readiness, and wait my word.
	But thou, meanwhile, relate what thou hast seen.
Gabriel	Our host went forth in radiant panoply,
	And soon we reached the regions of the earth.
	There we beheld the hosts of Antichrist
	Defying Thee; for all the race of man
	Seemed turned against us. Everywhere men toiled
	But not for Thee, to magnify Thy Name,
	Or do the bidding of Thine Holy Church.
	Nay, rather they seemed seeking their own ends.
	For some wrought with strange engines to constrain
	The elements to serve their impious will;
	Or else they sought, with vain presumptuous search,
	To pluck the secret from all hidden places
	And pry into the hearts of holy things,
	Profaning them, and lay their godless hands
	On mysteries unlawful for man's search;
	While others strove for wealth, and fame, and power,
	Going about the earth in fruitless toil,
	Wronging their neighbours, breaking Thy commands,
	And giving up their souls to vanities.
	We cried aloud, rebuking their ill deeds,
	And urged repentence; but of all mankind
	None seemed to pay the slightest heed to us.
	Then we beheld their mighty host drawn up

As if for battle; far as eye could see
Stretched the vast throng. It seemed that all the earth
Was covered with their hordes, a host in which
Men of all nations, seeming of all times,
Stood up against us—some in antique garb,
Some clad after the fashion of today.
Various their weapons, some with sword and shield,
Some seemed unarmed, or bore but in their hands
A pen, a book, or other harmless thing,
While some had strange devices unto us
Unknown, that made us fear we knew not what.
We gazed throughout the earth; in every land
Men toiled as was their wont; nothing seemed changed,
None saw we go to join that impious host,
And yet its numbers ever grew more great.
In righteous wrath then stepped before the host
Michael, our Captain, and in clarion tones
He bade the foes surrender: "Godless ones
Daring to lift your puny hearts and hands
Against Omnipotence! Eternal death
And everlasting torments were too light
A penalty for such impiety!
Yet the Most High, in His exhaustless mercy,
Bade me present these terms of peace to you:
Cast down your impious weapons and repent
In sackcloth and in ashes, bow ye down
Unto the very dust and humbly pray
For mercy. Vow by what is holiest
To do God's will and to accept His Faith,
Henceforward and forever. Then perchance—
Perchance your lives may even yet be spared.
But if ye fail in fealty and homage,
His bidding is to slay you with the sword,

And cast your souls into the Hinnom Vale,
The Outer Darkness and the Sea of Flame
Which is the Second Death! Do ye submit?"
But no one made reply, so we advanced
Upon them with drawn swords, and in the van
Our leader, Michael, radiant as the sun
In midmost heaven, his adamantine mail
Shed living flames, and his refulgent sword
Flashed like ten lightning flashes wreathed in one.
Our enemies stood firm, and did not show
One sign of rage, of hatred, or of fear:
Calm seemed they, as if conscious of their might,
And without aught save pity for their foes.
They raised no hand against us, but dark clouds
Began to rise between us; darkness fell
Upon the earth and covered all the field.
Still we advanced, although we could not see
The foes who stood hidden in murky veils.
But ere we reached them, here and there broke forth
Lightning, and thunders echoed near and far.
The flashes gave us glimpses of their host,
And, as we closer looked, our wondering eyes
Beheld the forms of mighty ones of old,
Men famed for virtue e'en in heathen times,
But foes unto our Lord. We thought that they
Long since had fallen to the depths of hell,
But now it seemed as if they led the world.
We saw not what they did, but here and there
Where fell the lightnings, shattered were our ranks;
Our stricken warriors fell on every hand.
But now more near those fearful streams of light
Blazed right before us, and our very souls
Seemed seared by them; fear crept into our hearts,

And we retreated, but, as we drew back,
A light flashed forth just where our leader stood.
No more we tarried; trembling with affright
We fled, but looking backward we beheld
Our leader, his sword broken, and his arms
Rent and disfigured, fall.

Phan.   What! Is our host
Then routed by the reptiles of the depths?

Gabriel Oh Lord, have mercy on us; I but tell
What Thou Thyself commanded, and no more
I know than I have told Thee of the fray,
E'en as mine eyes beheld it.

Phan.   All ye hosts
Of heaven, ye Principalities and Powers,
Angels, and Archangels, Celestial Thrones,
Ye Cherubim and Seraphim, arise
In arméd throngs behind me; 'tis the day
Appointed for the smiting of our foes.
Bring forth mine armour fashioned for this fray.

The Angels When Thou didst tread upon the earth
                   Among the men who die,
          Thou wert as one of mortal birth,
                   Though sprung from God most high.
          Helpless Thou wert, a little child,
                   To face a sinful world,
          And bear with patience meek and mild
                   The ills against Thee hurled.
          The Lord of Darkness tempted Thee
                   With gifts of worldly might,
          But Thou didst spurn his vanity
                   And kingdoms of the night.

Thou didst proclaim God's holy will,
    And heal the halt and blind,
That sinners yet might turn from ill
    And heavenly mercy find.
Thou borest all the pains of man
    From birth unto the grave,
And on the Cross fulfilled God's plan,
    Mankind from sin to save.
So, by that anguish passing thought,
    Endured so patiently,
Thy spirit's deathless arms were wrought,
    That now we bring to Thee.

Angels These greaves, that in Thine earthly days
bringing   The meekness of Thy life
greaves Prepared while treading humble ways,
    Shall guard Thee in the strife.

Angels This breastplate, that of old was wrought
bringing   By all Thy grievous woes,
breastplate And love divine, shall set at naught
    The weapons of Thy foes.

Angels The sword of righteousness divine
bringing   Now gird we at Thy side.
sword And when in strife that blade will shine,
    None may its stroke abide.

Angels The shield of innocence so white
bringing   We yield unto Thine hand,
shield To ward Thee from the godless might
    Of the unholy band.

Angels   The helmet of Thine holiness
bringing   We place upon Thy brow.
helmet   Thine enemies in sore distress
            Shall find no mercy now.

All Angels Holy, Holy, Holy,
           Thou Lord of endless might,
       Thine hosts assemble slowly
           And gather for the fight.
       To drive to hell's dark portals,
           Engulfing as the sea,
       The souls of sinful mortals
           Who will not worship Thee.

Phan.   Ye angel hosts, for twice a thousand years
       We waited for this day. It is at hand.
       The Man of Sin, the Godless Antichrist,
       The Scarlet Harlot, and the Beast of Hell,
       With all the hosts of darkness rise in might
       To claim dominion o'er the realms of earth.
       Our hosts are routed, Michael is o'erthrown,
       And servants of Apollyon rule the world.
       Therefore I lead the heavenly hosts to war.
       And, since the tribes of men have joined our foes,
       No longer will I spare them. I declare
       The days of Earth are ended; I this day
       Devote it to destruction; all its hosts
       I yield unto your hands. Let wind and wave
       And flood and fire with resistless might
       Consume it, blot it out, annihilate
       The den of wickedness, and send on men
       The woes of retribution for their sins.
       Ye angels of the trumpets, sound your blasts!

(Seven trumpet blasts sound in succession from different parts of the stage.
The scene grows dark, with lightning and thunder.)

The Angels   Woe to the tribes of earth and wicked men,
    To mighty hosts be woe.
The skies wax dark, earth seems a noisome fen,
    And streams with blood shall flow.

Phan.   Ye angels of the elements, unleash
The forces of destruction upon earth.

The Angels   The vials of wrath are emptied on mankind
    And all the ills of earth on them descend.
They seek the refuge they shall nowise find,
    And strive in vain to flee their destined end.

Phan.   Now, Gabriel, sound thy trumpet, and call forth
The resurrected dead to face their doom.

(Angels solemnly bring trumpet to Gabriel who takes it
and blows four blasts, one in each of the four directions,
North, East, South, and West. He returns trumpet to
angels. During the singing of the next chorus, hosts of
armed angels enter and stand behind Gabriel.)

The Angels   Ye mortals, who in death have lain
    From every nation, age, and clime,
Arise! the dooms of bliss or pain
    Await you at the end of time.
The trumpets sound: on every side
    The armies of the Lord advance.

THEY SUMMON   And think ye that the grave can hide
THE SOULS OF
THE DEAD   Your evils from his searching glance?
TO THE LAST   Awake! arise! Cast off the clay
JUDGEMENT   And naked face God's ruthless light.
Yet tremble if in any way
    Ye have transgressed eternal right!
Your hopes to hide within the tomb
    The records of your lives are vain.
This day unrolls the scroll of doom:
    Unending bliss or endless pain.

Gabriel   Great Lord, I bow in reverence before Thee,
          Then draw my sword,

                    (Draws sword)

                              which, in Thy Name I swear,
          Shall nevermore unto its sheath return
          While any being in the earth or sky
          Lives who adores Thee not. Behold! Our hosts
          In radiant armour wait upon Thy will.
          And in our hearts burns one intense desire
          To serve Thee, and wreak havoc on Thy foes.
          Now, Lord, we but await Thine holy word.

Phan.   Go, Gabriel, lead the vanguard of our host,
          And I myself will follow; 'tis the hour
          For which the ages yearned. The end is here.
          The grapes of wrath are ripe, doom's harvest stands
          And waits but for the reaping of our hands.

Gabriel   Ye hear the mandate of the Lord Divine:
          The hour hath come, the end of all the years,
          Just doom for all the hosts of wickedness.
          And now prepare to smite them! Draw your swords!
          Forward to battle in the name of God!

          *(Angels start marching from the scene. A vast host led by
          Gabriel is followed by a far vaster host led by Phantasmus.)*

Angels   Go forth, great Lord, to victory!
who   How can the creatures of Thine hands
remain   In madness strive themselves to free
behind   From Thine omnipotent commands?
          How can those wretches, born in sin,
                Whose lives are as a raindrop's fall,
          In deadly battle hope to win
                Against the mighty Lord of all?

For Thou art holy, Thou art wise,
    And Thou art mighty as the sun:
The foolish wicked who despise
    Thy will, shall find themselves undone,
And flee in terror at Thy might
    When, on this final day of Doom,
Thine host advances, clothed in light,
    To cast Thy foes to endless gloom.

We praise Thee, Who from the first hour,
Alone in Thine almighty power
    Didst sit above the silent world;
And, while the gloom of ancient night
Fled at the birth of primal light,
    Thine hands the firmament unfurled.
Then Thou didst form the formless earth,
And bring all living things to birth
    According to Thy wisdom's plan;
And, taking up the lowly clay,
Didst shed thereon a living ray
    To fashion forth the race of man.
What folly then for men to hope
Through their own strength with sin to cope,
    When all their fate lies in Thine hands?
Through Thee alone they came to live,
'Tis Thine to damn them or forgive,
    For naught prevails save Thy commands.
Yet weak, and blind, and most perverse,
These outlaws of the universe
    Dare to defy Thine holy will.
And, leagued with them in grim array,
The Lords of Darkness join the fray
    And cherish hopes of triumph still.

THEY PRAISE
THEIR LORD

But though the rebels, stern and bold,
As those who challenged Thee of old,
    In madness brave Thine awful might,
Swift wilt Thou smite them and o'erthrow
Their works of ill and cast them low
    From out the spaces of the light.

For all the angel hosts advance
    Against the demons from below;
And, facing war's uncertain chance,
    Prepare to answer blow by blow,
On Armageddon's sanguined field,
    Where Christ with Antichrist contends,
AND PREDICT Until the Godless host shall yield
HIS VICTORY   And scatter to creation's ends.
One struggle, one great shock of spears—
    The tide of conflict ebbs away,
And shouts of victory, and tears
    Of vanquished rebels close the day.
And then wilt Thou, in righteous wrath,
    On all the wicked host impose
Just doom, and drive them on the path
    That leads to never-ending woes.
Swift roll the clouds of gloomy fight
    Across the tracts of earth and sky.
We scarce behold the heavenly light;
    The din of conflict sounds more nigh.
And ever in the fiercest press
    Of strife, Thy weapons flame afar:
To foes a portent of distress,
    To all Thy friends a guiding star.

Yet Ah! We would turn from sterner things:
From the sounding battle that crashes and rings,
From the awful face of Thy righteous ire,
From Thine eyes of wrath and Thy sword of fire.
And our hearts yearn back through the mists of the past
    That dimly gleam in the dusk of the years,
Like the floods of an ocean, vague and vast,
    An ocean of terror, and travail, and tears,
To a milder, fairer, and sweeter day,
When the Holy Child in the manger lay.
Oh how can our lips in this latter time

THEY TURN
WITH NOSTALGIA
TO THE MEMORY
OF THE
NATIVITY

Sing the songs we sang with the stars in chime,
When the hosts of Heaven, the kings of Earth,
Rejoiced at Mary's stainless birth!
When the anthem that rang through the night so still
Was: "Peace on earth, unto men of good will!"
'Twas a flutter of wings through the dewy night,
A whisper of words, a glimmer of light:
The wings of the angels that hovered near,
The words of the shepherds in holy fear,
The light of the star that shone on high,
A beacon to all from far and nigh;
Where lay the Holy Infant so mild,
The Word of God made flesh in a child!
Ah! For the visions that shone so fair,

AND A VISION
OF SALVATION

The dawn of hope on a world's despair,
The hope of salvation for all mankind,
Of strength to the sick and sight to the blind,
And mercy to sinners bowed down with woe.
Alas, that visions so fair should go.
For evil men in their hate for Thee,
Reared the Cross upon desolate Calvary.
And the Church which Thy Blood established then,
Must war forever with sinful men

Who scorn Thy Name, and Thy faith despise,
Who trust alone to their earthly eyes.
And mankind seeks ever, with restless soul,
To reach and conquer some worthless goal.
Their toil and striving no respite brings,
They trade and traffic in transient things,
They find no peace for the soul's distress,
And fill themselves full of emptiness.
But we fain would forget these evil days
      And dream of a brighter and earlier time
When the earth was filled with Thine holy praise
      And faith was fair as the year's fresh prime.
And we long for the time when Thy vanquished foes
Will reap a harvest of condign woes,
      In just requital for lives of crime.
So we turn to Thee still in this darkened hour,
When shades of the tempest about us lour,
When worlds are shattered and all things fail,
In the trust that Thy mercy will yet prevail.

Leader of   What wild, fear-wingéd messenger is this?
Chorus   Methinks he bears a darkness to mine eyes.

          (Enter Second Messenger)

              What are thy tidings?
Mess.   All is lost.
Leader   All lost?
              What? Have the fiends of hell o'erthrown high God?
Mess.   He whom we called the Lord is fallen; the host
          We called the host of darkness wear the light.
Leader Thy words are wild, a shade swims 'round mine eyes,
          These adamantine-pillered halls of God
          Seem trembling to my sight as if a wind

Upturned the lofty turrets of the clouds!
The stars seem reeling from their spheres! Oh Christ,
Thou Lord Creator, art Thou then o'erthrown?

Mess. Alas, I know not, all my world is perished.
All that I knew hath passed away, what things
Now be I cannot fathom anywise.
For, were the utmost stars of highest Heaven
Whelmed in the nethermost depths of lampless Hell,
And earth and sea commingled with the skies
In one vast lawless ruin, there were scarce
Confusion in the world that could be matched
To what mine eyes beheld.

Leader   Ah, let us learn
The dreadful issue of that dolorous strife.

Mess. Our host advanced; celestial panoply
Ensheathed the limbs of all the warrior saints
And angels. Our Great Leader, whom we called
Lord God Creator, led the van and bore
That flaming sword beneath whose dint of yore
The Great Apostate, Satan, headlong fell
To the flaming pit, what time the embattled powers
Of Heaven smote the arméd hosts of Hell.
As we approached the field where conflict raged
We heard the din of battle: swords on shields
Made frightful clangor, and commingled cries
Seemed like the roaring of an angry sea.
Above us hung thick clouds as black as night,
Whence jagged lightnings leapt; while from the ground,
Vexed by the stormy turbulence of strife,
Dense clouds of dust arose which hid the field,
While streaks of mist and drifting wrack of clouds
Spread darkness like a curtain over all.
But soon that dim and sightless veil of night
Was drawn aside a moment, and our eyes

Beheld once more our foemen, but no more
Could we discern a sword, or shield, or spear;
Rather it seemed they fought with lightning-bolts,
With flames of fire, and streams of dazzling light.
Headlong we rushed to meet the foe, but plunged
Into the blank, impenetrable mists,
Wherein we could nor friend nor foe discern.
So we stood thwarted, helpless to advance.
Then the mists parted in the upper air,
Leaving the field still hidden, and disclosed
An iron sky, beneath which we beheld
Sheer rugged rocks touched with a strange red glow.
There, on the topmost crag, against the sky,
Stood forth two mighty forms: the One we knew,
Our Leader, girt with adamantine mail,
Holding aloft His yet-unconquered sword;
Fronting Him stood a maiden, armed, whose helm
And breastplate gleamed with radiance like the day,
And on her shield was blazoned the device
Of a snake-tresséd woman, stony-eyed,
While from the spear she bore within her hand
Shone dazzling light, beside whose intense gleam
The brightest effluence of the noonday sun
Or the clear light of our High Sovereign's face
Had seemed a sickly bale-fire of the marsh
Or pitch's flickering and much-smoking flame,
So awful was the splendour of that light.
Just as the two approached to join in strife,
A cloud of mist swept by, and for a space
All things were hidden both in earth and sky.
But when it passed, we saw the earth no more,
Naught but the sky with storm-clouds tempest-tossed,
Lit with wild levin-light, and in the midst,

An eagle and a serpent linked in strife.
Long raged the doubtful conflict; gleaming scales
Torn by sharp beak and talons fell like flakes
Of fire, and blood-stained plumes were strewn in air.
At length the serpent, writhing mightily,
Fixed his fell fangs full in the eagle's throat
Whose wings drooped nerveless, and his claws unclasped.
Like to a stone he fell through the dim air.
But wonderful to say, the serpent fell not!
Forth from his body wings of rainbow grain
Sprouted, upon his head a crown of light
Appeared, and rays as from the orb of day
Shot forth behind him. The dark clouds of night
Melted like shadows at the touch of morn.
Brighter and brighter grew the waxing light,
Until for very brightness, we no more
Beheld the crownéd serpent. Now the veils
Of gloom were wholly vanished, and we saw
Again the earth and all the mighty host.
But strange to tell, all seemed not as before—
For nowise could we friend from foe discern!
We saw no more the arméd lords of Hell
Nor our own leaders, nor was any hand
Or weapon raised against us. One vast host
In perfect concord covered all the earth:
Our foes and we seemed blended. When our eyes
Sought out the leaders, somehow it appeared
As if we knew them, as of our own host,
But not as erstwhile. Sudden a great cry
Rang forth, it seemed from all the host together:
"Let there be peace on earth forevermore,
As Truth and Wisdom have at last prevailed!"
And then within my heart I seemed to hear,

As echo to that cry, a voice which bade:
"Return, return, for Wisdom hath prevailed!"
Naught else remained to do; so I return,
With heavy heart and spirit sore perplexed.

The Angels   Alas for fields with fruitless battles red!
      Alas, for hopes that blossomed in despair!

THEY BEWAIL Alas for light that now from us hath fled,
THE END OF FAITH   And plunged us in a gloom we scarce can bear!
Alas for tears that all in vain are shed!
      Alas, for faith is dead!

(The Muses enter during the singing)

The Muses   Faith is not dead, it shall again arise,
But Wisdom, thronéd on the azure skies,

THEY HAIL   Shall lift Her lamp above
THE RETURN
OF WISDOM The clouds of doubt and terror that dismay,
While faiths of night shall perish in the day
      Of perfect Truth and Love.

The Angels   Who then are ye who sing of faith once more?

The Muses   We are of those who held these seats of yore,
      Ere ye attained the sky;
We wandered among tribes of alien birth,
We walked as exiles o'er the fields of earth,
      Banished from realms on high.
We saw the old world with its might and glory
      Perish amid a night of gathering gloom,
We saw primaeval things prove transitory,
      And earth o'erspread with shadows of the tomb.
But now at length the light of Truth returneth,
      The long, long night is o'er,
Faith re-enkindled like the sunrise burneth,
      And we return once more.

The Angels   What faith can be, when ancient faith is slain?
The Muses   A faith that holds no fables up to blind
          The eyes of Truth, and seeks not to enchain
             By iron rules the freedom of mankind;
          And strives no more by terrors to restrain
             The searchings of the mind.
          Not faith in any god whose laws decree
          That human souls are doomed eternally,
             By some mysterious plan,
          But faith in that clear light within the soul
THEY OUTLINE   Guiding the spirit to a glorious goal—
A RATIONAL FAITH   The faith of man in man.
          Faith that the Powers that purify and bless,
          As Wisdom, Love, and utter Righteousness,
             Shall rule forevermore—
          Faith that man yet shall conquer every ill,
          Faith in the final triumph of his will
             In harmony with law.
          Faith that no heights shall be beyond his scaling,
             Faith that his mind shall master change and chance,
          Faith that his strength, for every need availing,
             Shall vanquish every adverse circumstance.
          Faith in the splendid hopes his heart may cherish,
             Faith in his wisdom's might.
          Faith that all evil shapes of night shall perish,
             As darkness yields to light.

The Angels   But what befell you through the vanished years,
          And whence the hope that would surpass our fears?

The Muses   When him ye worshipped as the Lord Supernal,
                    Usurped the thrones and seats of ancient power,
              And rites of worship men believed eternal,
                    Were swept to nothingness in one brief hour,
              We wandered exiled from our native regions,
                    And walked the earth where darkness reigned once more,
              As ignorance and fear's unholy legions
                    O'erspread the realm where Wisdom ruled of yore.
              We saw the splendid lamps of ancient art

THEY RELATE   Quenched one by one and hidden from all sight,
THE EVENTS   We saw the worshippers of Truth depart
DURING THE   And Error seated on the throne of might,
TERM OF   While through a ruined world whose heart was broken
THEIR EXILE   We saw the altars of a shame unspoken
                    On every hand arise:
              The altars of a tyrant fell and cruel,
              The altars where men's souls were burned for fuel
                    To feed enthronéd lies.
              And whoso would not bow the knee to error
                    Was given over to avenging flame,
              While shadowy despair and ghostly terror
                    Filled earth with fear and shame.

AND OF THEIR But in the wildernesses of the mountains,
REFUGE IN THE   And by mysterious streams
WILDERNESS   Where pathless forests hid the secret fountains,
                    Men still dreamed holy dreams.
              And while most regions of the earth were pining
                    In darkness deeper than the deepest night,
              Within their starlike souls undimmed was shining
                    The ancient holy light.
              And by that light the reign of night is shaken,
                    Its shadows pass away,
              As freedom, hope, and gladness reawaken
                    In Truth's returning day.

The Angels   But where dwelt ye while those long years went by,
And who are these we see now drawing nigh?

(Enter the Gods)

The Gods   Far, far over ocean's waves
and the   Lies an ancient land,
Muses   Where a sacred river laves
           A golden strand,

IN A LAND   Where the holy lotus floats
THAT DID NOT   Through the tranquil hours,
ABANDON
THE WISDOM   And the zephyrs waft the notes
OF THE AGES   Of birds, and the perfume of flowers.

There the Gods who from Hellas were banished
           Abode on an alien shore,
And the Wisdom of ages long vanished
           Was cherished once more.
Though the priests of a creed benighted
           Laid waste the world with their rod,
And the peoples were driven affighted
           By a phantom they served as God.
Yet Wisdom's Lords abiding
           Beyond all sight,
Through mysterious ways were guiding
           To perfect light,
The race of men, who, having put behind them
           Folly and ignorance,
No more will suffer vain beliefs to blind them
           To Truth's advance.
And we, as victors in the strife compelling
           The hosts of night to flee,
Return in gladness to our ancient dwelling
           Triumphantly.

(*Enter Prometheus, Zeus, Pallas*)
(*The Angels, to Prometheus, seeing him as The Eternal Saviour*)

The Angels   Hail, Holy Lord, returning in Thy might!

The Spirits   Hail, Master of the realms of day and night
          And Sovereign of the worlds in endless flight!

The Muses   Hail, wisest Ruler of foreboding sight!

All   Take now Thy throne amid eternal light!

Prom.   Did I give man the sacred fire
        To be myself a king of man?
   Did I defy the Heavenly Sire
        In place of Him to bless and ban?
   Did I endure the pains unspoken:
        The vulture's beak, the fetters base,
   So that when shameful bonds were broken
        I might enslave the human race?
   Did I endure that greater anguish,
        To dwell with those of mortal birth,
   Like them in helplessness to languish,
        And then presume to rule the earth?
   Though freed from chains by hero's hands
        And from unuttered agony,
   I still was chained by viewless bands,
        Until the human race was free!
   For how could I return to light
        While those I would have died to save
   Were victims of a tyrant's might
        And thought was superstition's slave?

But now the triumph of the powers
    Of wisdom brings us here once more,
When, after countless wretched hours,
    We claim the seats we held of yore.
But not as in those days long past!
    The bitter sorrows I have known
Have made me see the truth at last,
    And never will I take a Throne!
Yea, I have suffered, I have learned;
    Wisdom I bought, nor grudge its cost—
For freedom of mankind I yearned—
    And shall that freedom now be lost?
Therefore, O Zeus, since Thou likewise
    Hast purchased wisdom through distress,
Resume Thy throne, for Thou art wise,
    And Wisdom's reign is righteousness.

The Angels, on beholding Zeus under the aspect of The Eternal Father)

The Angels   Hail, Heavenly Father! Whom our Master sought
    In vain for endless years!
We know the mighty works Thine hands have wrought
    And put aside our tears,
Having at last beheld the consummation
    Of hopes surpassing fears,
The splendid vision of the world's salvation
    That to our eyes appears!

The Spirits   Hail, Mighty Power, whose ascendant star
    Our eyes beheld unnumbered years ago,
The final triumph we foresaw afar
    Through Thee achieved in this same hour we know.

The Muses   Hail, Thou our Father and our rightful King!
        Whose will is justice and eternal right,
    Reigning forever, to perfection bring
        The synthesis of mercy, truth, and might!

Zeus   My children, this is a far happier day
        Than when we last beheld this ancient hall,
    When dim forebodings of unreason's sway
        Lay on our spirits like a leaden pall.
    Adversity a clearer mind imparts,
        And, by the bitter ways we walked so long,
    This timeless truth lies graven on our hearts:
        Only by suffering Gods and Men grow strong.
    Therefore I will not take this lofty throne,
        Nor sit as sovereign of the subject skies.
    Lordship should rest in Wisdom's hands alone.
        Thou, Pallas, who art Wisdom's Self, arise,
    Take thou this throne and reign on high forever
        By thought's supreme, insuperable might.
    May Knowledge be the crown of all endeavour,
        And boundless space be filled with wisdom's light.

Pallas   I will not sit upon the seat of power
    For wisdom's triumph shall be freedom's hour.
    Lo! I am Science. In my hands I hold
    The key to nature's secrets manifold.
    Beneath my feet, the springs of night and day,
    And all things else are subject to my sway.
    I pierce the trackless void with boundless sight
    And weigh the utmost stars in endless night,
    I scale the heights, I plumb the deepest sea,
    And neither height nor depth hide aught from me.
    I wield a might that can remould the world
    Or shatter it to dust, in ruin hurled.

I know the truths by life and death concealed
And all their secrets are to me revealed.
Omniscience and omnipotence combine
To fix the boundless power that is mine.
My wisdom grasps the universal plan
And this I yield unto the hand of man.
My hand extends the lamp of Truth Divine,
Of which the piercing radiance shall shine
Throughout the spaces of the universe,
And, with the light of knowledge, shall disperse
Forevermore the darkness of the world.
Now let the scroll of nature be unfurled!
But what are worlds, though countless as the sands?
What is the might that nature's might commands?
And what are life and death with all their powers
But fading phantoms of the fleeting hours?
These things are shadows, spectres, shapes unsure,
Of which not e'en a vestige shall endure.
They are but dreams of the Eternal Mind,
And, passing, leave but memories behind.
While the Eternal Mind itself abides
Unchanged above illusion's shifting tides.
Eternal thought is changeless, sure, and free,
And man partakes of thought's eternity!

The Spirits   Hail, source of laws that endless worlds rehearse!

The Angels   Hail, Light of Truth, all shadows to disperse!

The Muses   Hail, Sovereign Wisdom of the Universe!

Pallas   So, having now achieved the consummation
     Of patient labour and unfaltering hope,
The Cosmos stands in utter integration,
     Comprised in systems of unbounded scope.
No more shall rash ambition reach for power;
     No more shall doubts delude nor fears dismay.
No more shall envy gnaw, nor greed devour,
     Nor tyranny oppress men, or betray.
The Gods shall dwell in harmony and beauty,
     As glad co-workers with the Cosmic plan,
And men, at last, accepting truth and duty,
     Achieve the glorious dignity of Man—
Worlds, of Divine Ideas the true reflection,
     With every being playing well its part,
Eternal growth to more complete perfection,
     And endless progress to Love's infinite heart!

The Muses   A Universe so great
     Our songs should celebrate!
So, let us join our voices and our lyres!
     But trust no partial view
     To part the false from true,
Clear seeing many diverse views requires.
     That portion we behold
     Then, let our words unfold,
So from all sides our thoughts like light may play,
     And all the veils that hide
     Be lifted quite aside,
'Til truth stands bare to knowledge as to day.

The Spirits   Flow on, oh sea of time
            To thy resistless tides,
      Awhile the stars keep chime,
            But none of them abides.
      They are, and are no more,
            Time's ocean, as it rolls,
      Keeps sweeping on its shore
            Atoms, and stars, and souls.
      In gardens of the sky
            Like flowers they bloom and fade:

THE SPIRITS
OF NATURE,
AS THE VOICE
OF SCIENCE,
DESCRIBE
THE ULTIMATE
REALITY AS
UNIVERSAL
ENERGY

      Like sparks they gleam and die,
            And vanish into shade.
      But through these endless changes,
            Energy's laws control
      The plan that multiplicity arranges
            Into an ordered whole.

      E'en as a breath that comes and goes
      The flood of Energy outflows,
      E'en as the beating of a heart
      In pulses aeon-tides apart.
      For, as that ancient sage* surmised
            That Love's and Strife's alternate reign
      All diverse things to one comprised,
            Then scattered them apart again,
      So, Energy from out the void
            Kinetic springs, and far and near
      Atoms and systems undestroyed
            Throughout all realms of space appear;
      But, as the cycle ends once more,
            The mighty fabrics cease to be,
      As energy all things withdraw
            Into potentiality.

* Empedocles.

Oh holy, all-embracing energy,
Which ever was, and ever yet shall be,
    The world is but a shadow of its might.
The changing shapes that vanish endlessly,
    Live only in its light.
For, whether systems rise or pass from being,
    Unchanged amid the changefulness of things,
As power and purpose evermore decreeing
        The planned perfection whence their order springs,
            Energy constant stands
            Amid Time's shifting sands,
Manifest agent of the Unseen Cause
            By which Creative Power
            Can form a world or flower,
And govern changing things by changeless laws.

The Angels   Earth, water, fire, and air,
            The face of heaven most fair,
All things that man holds splendid and sublime,
        Shall cease to be and pass
        As shadows in a glass,
Or clouds that drift above the sea of time.
        Though transient things decay,
        In endless truth shall stay
That which, not fashioned like the things that go,
        Shall evermore remain
        Though worlds and systems wane,
Above, beyond the ceaseless ebb and flow.
        Yea, though all nature dies
        And fades from changing skies,
The Power that moves outlives the cosmic frame.
        Unaltered It abides
        The flow of endless tides,

And through all future time shall be the same.
A changeless Purpose stands
Above Time's shifting sands,
The high directing Providence Divine;
That, with enfolding love
Forever stands above
The Universe to temper and refine.
And heavenly harmonies,
Devotion's sympathies,
Bring order out of chaos and decree
That stuff and strength and strife
Shall quicken into life,
And bloom as spirit in eternity.

The Muses Unmeasured nebulas of fire
And suns, the quintessence of light,
Planets that gem the sky's attire
And comets blazing through the night,
Across unbounded aether hurled—
What are they but an atom's heart?
Some fragment of a greater world
Itself in vaster frames a part?

AS THE VOICE
OF PHILOSOPHY,
THE MUSES
RELATE BOTH
THE PHENOMENAL
AND SUPER-
PHENOMENAL
ASPECTS
OF REALITY
TO SOMETHING
TRANSCENDING
THEM BOTH

Infinite matter, infinite mind,
With infinite energy combined,
Weave the vast web of being, wrought
With warp and woof of force and thought,
On looms whose threads are streams of light,
And shuttles, fire-trailing stars.
But is there naught beyond the night,
Beyond the endless gloom that bars
The utmost reach of aching sight,
But matter, mind, and energy?
Doth naught exist beyond these three?

Or is there something still unknown,
      Beyond the loom of nights and days,
      Beyond the maze of starry ways,
Beyond old night's primaeval throne?

Something that is not soul or mind,
      Something that is not force or frame,
Something that boundless, unconfined,
By thought supernal scarce divined,
      Is more than form or name.
A Self beyond all selves, the source
      Of mind and matter, day and night.
Not force, but still the cause of force—
      A darkness that transcends all light,
      Beyond the utmost reach of sight.
Unknown, unknowable and still
The hidden fountain of the will
That through the star-strewn wildernesses
      Sends forth its ever-widening rays,
By which the cosmos still expresses
      The impulse that its growth obeys,
While stars and systems rise and fall
      And peopled planets run their rounds
Throughout the universal All,
      'Til life in every shape abounds.
Then endless progress shall at last
      Permit the race of man to know
The boundless Wisdom of the past,
      And, with the future's promise, grow
To face unmoved the final hour
      Of worlds that perish, and arise,
By Godlike Wisdom's holy power,
      To mastery of the infinite skies.

The Spirits   Fair is sensation and pleasant
                     The things that it brings to man:
                 A source of joy that is present
                     In all that the eye may scan,
                 In all that the ear may hear,
                     In all that the tongue may taste,

                 In the odours from far and near
                     As of blossoms amid the waste;
                 And in all one may touch with his hands
                     And may feel of the fullness of earth,
                 Of the wealth of the seas and the lands
                     And the blessings of gladness and mirth.

                 Fair is the world, and its splendours
                     Of colour and form without end:
                 Of what light to vision renders
                     Of all that its beams may lend,
                 The glory of snow-capped mountains,
                     The far-spreading rays of the morn,
                 The shimmer of light on the fountains,
                     And shining where daylight is born;
                 The cool green gloom of forest ways,
                     The mists and the clouds on high,
                 The gorgeous tints of sunset rays
                     That burn in the western sky.
                 And the stars in the infinite vastness
                     Of night when the winds are low,
                 And the world, to its uttermost fastness,
                     Shines forth in a glittering show.

Fair too are the myriad forms of earth,
  Of air, and of wave, and of flame,
And all that within them comes to birth
  To share of the life of the same,
With all the beauty of living things,
  From grass to trees and flowers,
From the flash of fins, or feet, or wings,
  To man's own Godlike powers,
And all his beauty and might, the clear
  Lithe strength that grapples the world,
His courage that mocks at fear
  With defiance at darkness hurled,
And the glorious works of his art and skill
  In tone, and colour, and form,
And his thought, that conquers, to serve his will,
  The lightning, the wave, and the storm.

The Angels   Fair is emotion and holy,
                 A golden chain that unites
               The soul of man most lowly
                 With Lords of the ultimate heights:
               The thrill of an unknown terror,
                 The pulse of an unknown joy,
THEY EXTOL   The hope that surpasses error,
THE BLISSES OF   The bliss without alloy,
FEELING AND   The longing for what he knows not,
ASPIRATION   The yearning for formless things,
               The vague desire that shows not
                 The source whence its being springs;
               The feeling of mystical power
                 Beyond what was known before,
               And love, the burning flower
                 That springs from the heart's deep core;

The sense of complete communion
 When man and God are one,
The rapture of perfect union
 When the pilgrimage is done;
And the ultimate ecstasy
 Of a ransomed soul's release,
When being itself dissolves, set free
 In a swoon of passionless peace.

The Muses   Fair is thought, and the powers
 That fashion the form of the skies
That rule the harmonious hours
 And prosper the works of the wise
That enter the deepest recesses
 Of Nature's inviolate shrine,
And bare, to the spirit's caresses,
 The heart of her secret divine,
That build, through the numberless ages,
 The fabrics of order and right,

THEY GLORIFY
THE SPLENDOURS
OF THOUGHT AND
CONTEMPLATION

And grasp, as the goal of the sages,
 The oneness of beauty and might,
That soar past the realms of the senses
 To regions of essences pure,
Where Being, unbodied, commences
 A reign that shall ever endure,
That reach to a formless perfection,
 Eternal, unchanging, and free,
Where uncircumscribed intellection
 Is one with whatever there be,
In a place where no sun ray nor moon ray
 Nor planet nor star sheds its gleams,
But a radiance fairer than noon ray
 Fills all with unquenchable beams;

No gloom with that splendour can mingle,
 No shadow or stray of the night,
The light of that region is single,
 For truth is the light!
There the strife and the travail of forces,
 The conflict of worlds and their Gods,
As they meet in the midst of their courses,
 And the universe trembles and nods,
Shall be known but as light that proceedeth
 From atoms at war in a flame.
While the discord forever recedeth,
 The harmony still is the same.
There the values of earth hold no longer
 As opposites relative still:
More or less, great or small, weaker, stronger,
 Light or dark, high or low, good or ill.
And beyond all these forms of illusion
 The Ultimate Essence is known,
That resolves every seeming confusion
 To Truth, absolute and alone.

The Spirits

THEY FORETELL
THE MATERIAL
ACHIEVEMENTS OF
FUTURE
HUMANITY

But the men of that realm of glory—
 In what shall they show their might?
Shall they shine like the chiefs of story
 As stars through the clouds of fight?
Shall they sit upon thrones made splendid
 With jewels that brightly blaze,
While legions of slaves, low-bended,
 Obey them and sound their praise?
Or perchance shall it be their pleasure
 Far, far o'er the dim sea-ways
To seek, in the merchant's treasure,
 The harvest of toilsome days?

Nay, the treasure they seek shall be knowledge,
    And wisdom their throne of light,
And the only slave they acknowledge
    Be nature's undisciplined might,
While as warriors they shall be braver
    Than those of past ages of strife,
For their foe shall be something far graver—
    A threat to Humanity's life.
Yea, the ones who shall bid defiance
    To the treacherous foes of mankind
Are the Godlike men of Science,
    The Lords of the Realms of Mind,
The Masters of Truth, strong and daring,
    With gaze unmoved at the skies.
The light of the Infinite glaring
    Shall blind not their fearless eyes.
There is naught that shall make them cower,
    There is naught that shall do them harm.
They shall wield irresistible power
    By Wisdom's invincible charm.
Neither heights nor depths shall appall them,
    They are masters wherever they go;
To the threat of what'er may befall them
    They can answer: "Yea, we know."
For they know the song that was sung
    By the morning stars of the prime
When the silence of space found tongue
    In the flowing rhythms of time.
And they know the ways of the wind
    And the paths of the stars on high,
The mysterious laws of the mind,
    And the secrets of sea and of sky.

They shall banish from earth the impureness
    Of selfishness, greed, lust, and rage,
And establish, in order and sureness,
    The base of a new Golden Age;
While the demon of war's desolations
    The strength of their Wisdom shall bind
In a Holy Union of Nations,
    A Commonwealth of Mankind.
All the dungeons and thrones of transgression
    Shall pass like the shadows of night,
As tyranny's darkest oppression
    Is vanquished by Liberty's light.
And, pure of all evil infection,
    Life, beautiful, joyous, and free,
Shall build of the body's perfection
    Fit shrine for the Godhead to be.

The Angels   The solace of religion yet
    Shall comfort men, but not confined
By any church or creed to set
    A bound to freedom of the mind.
For all the faiths of darker years,
    Like stars that gem the evening skies,

IN A UNIVERSAL
RELIGION
FAITH SHALL BE
AT ONE WITH
WISDOM,
AND FEAR SHALL
BE NO MORE

Through shades of folly, grief, and fears,
    Shine bright, 'till Wisdom's sun arise.
But when that sun puts forth its light,
They pale, they fade, they vanish quite.
    The sun shall rise, the stars shall fade,
The shadows of the night depart,
    And dismal phantoms of the shade
From out the light in terror start;
For light shall fill the human heart,
    And man no more shall be afraid.

THE GODS SHALL
BE AT PEACE,
Cronus and Zeus in peace shall reign,
  And let mankind be free,
While great Prometheus once again
  Beholds their harmony.

AND MEN
KNOW THEIR
TRUE NATURE
The many Gods that men adored
  Shall all be known in truth and right
As Virtue's ultimate reward
  And agencies of ordered might.
And That, the One, apart, above,
  In nothing yet in everything,
Whose way is universal love,
  To serve the All, not reign as king:
Not in the gloom of stately fanes,
  Nor in the heavens, void and wide,
Its Grace in human hearts remains,
  Its Works in human minds abide,
While filled with light, each human soul
  As Buddha and as Christ shall shine—
Boundless devotion to the Whole,
  Compassion endless and divine.

AND FOLLOW THE
PATH OF VIRTUE
And men, pursuing virtue's ways,
  Unchecked by creed, or race, or name,
Shall not be led by hope of praise,
  Nor driven by the fear of blame.
In Universal Brotherhood
  Shall all the tribes of earth unite—
Alike promote the general good,
  Alike uphold the common right.

The Muses

THEY DESCRIBE
AN ENDLESS VISTA
OF PROGRESS
Though man's dim vision may behold
  But clouds that veil the spirit's sight,
Beyond the clouds, the deeps unfold
  The stars of Wisdom's perfect light.

And he shall reach those stars, but find
    In them another world, with bars
To vision of the selfsame kind:
    Remoter clouds and loftier stars.

THE FUTILITY
OF RITUALISM

But he shall not attain that height
    By bending knee in any shrine,
Nor bowing at the altars bright
    With candles, nor where sunbeams shine,
Stained with fair hues from blazoned pane,
    Nor where slow incense-wreaths ascend
From golden censors in the fane,
    And organ-tones and voices blend
Their harmonies to fill the soul
    With yearnings for ecstatic flight—
For know: perfection's final goal
    Is not attained by any rite.

THE FOLLY
OF ASCETICISM

Think not that tortures of the frame,
    Scourgings or fastings can avail
To free the spirit from the shame
    That self-indulgences entail.
For pain and penance can not save
    The soul that struggles, weak and blind,
Since to enfeeble and enslave
    The body does not free the mind.

THE LIMITATIONS
OF MYSTICISM

Think not that ecstasies of soul,
    The visions of supernal things,
Of cosmic harmonies that roll,
    Of lights, and choirs, and angel wings,
Can lift one from the dismal doom
    Of those who tread the weary round
Between the cradle and the tomb
    Beside the dim abyss profound.

For man a centre is, where flow
 The forces that control the world—
His sole salvation is to know
 The secrets in his Selfhood furled,

THE SECRET IS
SELF-KNOWLEDGE

To find in Self the source of bliss,
 To find in self the cause of woe;
For Wisdom's noblest crown is this:
 The truest, highest Self to know!

THE MEANS OF
ITS ATTAINMENT,
AND THE ETERNAL
SUPREMACY
OF WISDOM

To seek the Self, and yet not selfish be—
 Though good, to hold not ill a thing apart—
To love all forms of life, and yet be free
 From thirst of life, and nowise set one's heart
On any earthly thing, for this shall pass
 And perish like the fading of a flower,
Swift as the fleeting shadows in a glass,
 Or sunset hues that vanish in an hour.
For, as a cloud in the Western sky,
 That the beams of departing day
With a transient radiance dye
 Ere they fade away,
Is the glory in wisdom not founded,
 A splendour that is not, but seems,
That fades in the darkness unbounded
 Like shadows of dreams.
But Truth is a mountain fastness,
 Crowned with eternal snow,
That stands unmoved in its vastness
 By the tumult below.
For the tempest can not overcome it
 And the avalanche plunges in vain,
While the sun rays guild the summit
 Beyond the clouds and the rain.

Or, like a star in a lofty place,
  Remote, undimmed by the night,
That far through the endless fields of space,
  Unceasing sheds its light.
Though worlds arise and are shattered
  Like foam on the waves of the sea,
Though the wrecks of lost systems are scattered
  On the shores of eternity,
Yet the star shines in splendour supernal,
  Untouched by time's fluctuant tides,
And the glory of Wisdom Eternal
  Forever abides.

All Oh man, in whom all diverse things unite
  From depths the lowest to the highest height,
MAN IS THE
MASTER OF THE He holds the mightiest power in his hands
COSMOS And subtlest forces yield to his commands.
A king is he, whose will all things obey;
Even life and death are subject to his sway.
Both seen and unseen worlds his realm shall be
O'er which he rules by Wisdom's mastery—
Knowledge his crown, the Universe his throne,
His sceptre Power, but power for good alone!

The Spirits Man, master of things material,
  Shall spread his supreme domain
From earth unto realms siderial
  In Wisdom's unlimited reign;
MAN SHALL
MASTER THE He shall follow all things to their sources,
MATERIAL WORLD The great and the small set at one,
And Nature's most recondite forces
  Be clear to his eyes as the sun.

He shall balance the forces that scatter,
 In patterns by Wisdom designed,
And place o'er the crudeness of matter
 The gracious control of the mind.
As an artist with sure precision
 Can form from the plastic clay
Whatsoever his mind may vision,
 And it needs must obey,
So thought's harmonious power
 Shall fashion the world anew,
And all man's hopes shall flower,
 And all of his dreams come true.
The dreams of the ancient sages:
 The stone that turns base things to gold,
The power to live through the ages
 And all of their wonders behold.
No longer shall earth restrain him,
 No bounds shall be set to his flight,
No finite domain shall contain him
 In the infinite ocean of night.
He shall cross that ethereal ocean
 To wander in realms afar,
And swift as thought or emotion
 He shall travel from star to star,
While the stars with their planets surrounded
 Shall help him his hope to fulfill,
And the whole of the Cosmos unbounded
 Acknowledge the strength of his will.
Though the systems themselves are dissolving
 Like bubbles that come and go,
And pass with the cycles revolving,
 As the world-tides ebb and flow,

Yea, though all things else have their ending
  And the skies like a scroll are furled—
Though the ultimate darkness descending
  As night shall possess the world—
Yet man, by his wisdom supernal,
  Shall pass from the temporal clime
To abide in a region eternal,
  Untouched by the ruins of time.

The Angels Man, Lord of the heart's desire,
  Shall ever unmoved remain
By passion's insidious fire,
  Or impulse of pleasure or pain.
No delights of the senses shall draw him
  To wander from temperate ways,

MAN SHALL
MASTER FEELINGS, No menace or terror shall awe him
DESIRES, AND
PASSIONS
  Or unforeseen issues amaze.
No anger or hatred shall blind him
  Or bias his judgement's keen eyes,
No pride or ambition shall bind him
  To actions unjust or unwise.
No sorrow or grief can depress him
  Or make him lose sight of his goal,
No remorse or despair can distress him
  Who has mastered supreme self-control.
No ecstasy, yearning, or rapture
  Can stir the deep stillness within
His repose, which no longings can capture,
  Or tempt him to folly or sin.

AND BECOME A   Yet love in his spirit shall flourish,
PERFECT CHANNEL
FOR IMPERSONAL
LOVE
  A clear and luminous flame—
No evil his heart shall nourish,
  No shape of unreason or shame,

But the love, without fear or repression,
    That fills and illumines his soul,
Shall reach its most perfect expression
    In Brotherhood, linking the Whole.
That ideal of all beings as brothers
    No selfish pursuit shall alloy,
As he finds, in the service of others,
    The highest fulfillment of joy.
He shall rise from ecstatic devotion
    To the splendour of visible things,
With a purer and nobler emotion,
    As Love helps the soul grow her wings.
He shall pass from the worship of Beauty
    In forms by the senses divined,
To discern, in devotion to Duty,
    A loveliness born of the mind,
From the grace apprehended in feeling
    To the glory of Truth understood—
From the Primal Ideas, self-revealing,
    To the absolute love of The Good.
His devotion and thought shall discover
    A sunrise of spirit most bright,
As Love, and Belovéd, and Lover
    Are One in the fullness of light!

The Muses Man, Master of Thought Supernal,
    Shall rule in a realm most high;
He shall govern with laws eternal

BY THOUGHT
MAN SHALL
MASTER THE
PROCESS OF
COSMIC CREATION

    The powers of earth and sky:
Far, far in the distant regions
    Where ancient worlds have died,
Where clouds of stars, as legions
    Of light, in the void abide—

Where Time, and Stillness, and Spaces
    Of Darkness possess the All—
Where the outposts of chaos, in places
    Of silence, await the call—
The call of Creative Power
    That shall waken another Day—
That shall send, at its destined hour,
    A world reborn on its way—
That shall quicken the dim abysses
    With stirrings of life and love,
As Being, and Knowledge, and Blisses
    Reflect the perfection above.
For Thought is the power transcendent
    That calls from the vastness afar,
The aspect of Truth resplendent
    In atom, and soul, and star.
And e'en in man are the forces
    That summon new systems to light,
For his mind is one with the sources
    Of world-building might.

All   Man, Lord of a Wisdom far-seeing,
       Abides, as appearances fade.

MAN
SHALL ATTAIN
THE WISDOM
THAT REVEALS TO
HIM THE REALITY
BEHIND COSMIC
PROCESSES AND
ITS ACTION BY
PRINCIPLES OF

REEMBODIMENT,

He shall fathom the fabrics of Being
    And find them less real than a shade.
He shall see them, dissolving and shattered,
    Resuming the state whence they came,
As their wrecks o'er the Cosmos are scattered,
    And they vanish, blown out like a flame.
He shall see them return in due season,
    Embodied in forms that provide,
In the patterns of Justice and Reason,
    Experience ever more more wide.

CAUSATION,
He shall know how all cosmic reactions
  Are bound by a law that decrees
That the sequence of causative actions
  Restore the disturbed harmonies.

INTERRELATION,
He shall see how all beings are Brothers,
  Where each, through its self-attained rôle,
Finds its proper relation to others,
  And its place in a unified whole.

ESSENTIAL CHARACTERISTIC,
He shall know how each being acquires
  True Selfness, whereby it displays
Its own self-devised aims and desires,
  Its own individual ways.

INVOLUTION AND EVOLUTION,
He shall see how in ceaseless progression
  Forms appear and dissolve o'er and o'er,
As their essence in form finds expression,
  And the forms become essence once more.

THE PATH OF COMPASSIONATE SERVICE,
He shall learn of the choice between reaching
  A bliss to one's selfhood confined,
And the selfless devotion to teaching
  And helping all beings combined.

AND SELF-KNOWLEDGE
He shall know That which is before any
  Illusions of aspect or name,
How The One manifests as The Many,
  And yet is forever the same.

THUS ATTAINING COMPLETE ENLIGHTENMENT AND ULTIMATE PERFECTION
On the wheel of the ages returning,
  In cycles of days beyond date,
He shall garner the harvest of learning
  The meaning of Cause, Time, and Fate.
He shall rise in eternal ascension
  Forever and ever more high—
From a vast to a vaster dimension,
  From sky to more infinite sky,

With a Wisdom that ever increases,
 At one with life's limitless sea,
Compassion whose scope never ceases,
 More pure and more deep and more free—
The Lord of ineffable power—
 The Crown of an infinite plan—
Eternity's ultimate flower:
 The Spirit of Man!

THE BRIDGE BUILDER

THE BRIDGE BUILDER

Pontifices the Romans named
    Their priests: Bridge Builders; for they wrought
A bridge 'twixt Gods and Mortals, framed
    Of rite and legend, deed and thought.
Bridge Builder in a later year
    Am I, who, seeking still the true,
With woven words essay to rear
    A bridge between the old and new.
Far off, across the stream of time,
    The light of ancient Hellas gleams;
And latter ages, less sublime,
    Are guided by those distant beams.
Between, as black as midnight sea,
    Ages of darkness roll their tides.
By that dim waste the light may be
    Obscured, but still the light abides.
The light that shone in ancient Greece
    Shall in our times once more arise,
And match the younger years' increase
    With vaster worlds in vaster skies.
I do but strive, in night and storm,
    To stretch a slender span aright.
Let those a firmer fabric form
    Who labour in the morning light!
For still the wildered wanderer needs
    To reach the light that shines afar,
Where, through the storm of warring creeds,
    Truth gleameth as a guiding star.